THE TRIAL OF CHARLES I

THE **BROADVIEW**
SOURCES SERIES

The Trial
of Charles I

edited by K.J. KESSELRING

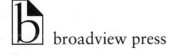 broadview press

BROADVIEW PRESS – www.broadviewpress.com
Peterborough, Ontario, Canada

Founded in 1985, Broadview Press remains a wholly independent publishing house. Broadview's focus is on academic publishing; our titles are accessible to university and college students as well as scholars and general readers. With over 600 titles in print, Broadview has become a leading international publisher in the humanities, with world-wide distribution. Broadview is committed to environmentally responsible publishing and fair business practices.

The interior of this book is printed on 100% recycled paper.

Library and Archives Canada Cataloguing in Publication

The trial of Charles I / edited by K.J. Kesselring.

(Broadview sources series)
Includes bibliographical references.
ISBN 978-1-55481-291-2 (paperback)

1. Charles I, King of England, 1600-1649—Trials, litigation, etc.—Sources. 2. Charles I, King of England, 1600-1649—Death and burial—Sources. 3. Trials (Treason)—Great Britain—History—17th century—Sources. 4. Regicides—Great Britain—History—17th century—Sources. 5. Great Britain—History—Charles I, 1625-1649—Sources. I. Kesselring, Krista J., 1972-, editor II. Series: Broadview sources series

DA396.A22T75 2016   941.06'2   C2016-900800-2

Broadview Press handles its own distribution in North America
PO Box 1243, Peterborough, Ontario K9J 7H5, Canada
555 Riverwalk Parkway, Tonawanda, NY 14150, USA
Tel: (705) 743-8990; Fax: (705) 743-8353
email: customerservice@broadviewpress.com

Distribution is handled by Eurospan Group in the UK, Europe, Central Asia, Middle East, Africa, India, Southeast Asia, Central America, South America, and the Caribbean. Distribution is handled by Footprint Books in Australia and New Zealand.

Broadview Press acknowledges the financial support of the Government of Canada through the Canada Book Fund for our publishing activities.

Edited by Juliet Sutcliffe
Book Design by Em Dash Design

PRINTED IN CANADA

CONTENTS

ACKNOWLEDGEMENTS

My thanks to Professors Sears McGee and Brian Cowan and to the third anonymous reviewer of this volume's proposal, as well as to the anonymous reviewer of the completed manuscript, for their helpful advice. Thanks, too, to Dr. Patrick Ludolph for sharing a copy of his recently completed doctoral dissertation on Gilbert Mabbott. I am also very grateful to Abigail McInnes, who read through the draft to spot points that students might need explained. Special thanks go as well to the librarians and archivists who helped secure the images used in this volume and provided permission to publish them, including staff at the Parliamentary Archives and the British Library. I am especially indebted to Karen Smith, the rare books librarian at my own institution's Killam Library, and fortunate that we have as rich and well-tended a collection of early modern works as we do.

INTRODUCTION

In January of 1649, after years of civil war, King Charles I stood trial in a specially convened English court on charges of treason, murder, and other "high crimes" against his people. Kings had lost their crowns before, in battles or aristocratic coups, but here a king faced a public prosecution for his actions. Not only did the revolutionary tribunal find Charles guilty and order his death, but its masters then abolished monarchy itself and embarked on a bold (if short-lived) republican experiment. In a speech given on the 350th anniversary of King Charles's execution, the Honourable Justice Michael Kirby called the trial "a discreditable affair" by legal standards. He also argued, however, that it "established a principle, written in the king's blood, which altered for all time the character of the monarchy, the parliament, and the relations between each." It had profound and far-reaching consequences, this Australian judge observed, that "resound even today throughout the world. They underlie the rights of the people which give ultimate legitimacy to the constitutional arrangements in countries still unknown when the king faced his end."[1] At the very least, the trial represented a watershed in English political history and theory, and thus also affected subsequent developments in those parts of the world colonized by the British.

Monarchs no longer dominate forms of political organization as they once did. Over the nineteenth and twentieth centuries, revolutionaries and reformers abolished many monarchies in favour of forms of government justified on democratic or republican principles. Where monarchies persist, they do so more often under constitutional limits than with absolute or autocratic powers. Europe's remaining monarchies—three of which still reign over parts of the Americas (including, of course, Canada)—are firmly fettered by formal legal restraints, for example. Monarchies with more robust powers continue in the Gulf States and Middle East. Japan, Thailand, Swaziland, and other countries, too, retain monarchs, with varying degrees of effective power. Most countries, however, now do without.

This modern shift away from royal regimes of inherited power focused on one individual (usually a man) would have amazed many an early modern observer. One sixteenth-century political philosopher observed that "all the laws of nature point toward monarchy," a sentiment that would have seemed common place and common sense to many in his own day.[2] While they had examples of other forms of government in their histories and Bibles, and a few small instances of republican rule in continental Europe, most early modern English people would have seen monarchy as a fact ordained by God, by nature, and by human law. And, indeed, England has a limited form of monarchical government even today. Yet

---

1   The Hon. Justice Michael Kirby, "The Trial of King Charles I: Defining Moment for Our Constitutional Liberties," (Anglo-Australasian Lawyers' Association, Great Hall, Gray's Inn, London, 22 January 1999): www.hcourt.gov.au/assets/publications/speeches/former-justices/kirbyj/kirbyj_charle88.pdf

2   Jean Bodin, *Six Books of the Commonwealth*, trans. M.J. Tooley (Oxford: Oxford UP, 1955), 199.

it was the early modern English—or some of them, at least—who decided to put a king on public trial, to execute him as a traitor to his people, and then to abolish the monarchy. Though their own republican period proved short lived, it had repercussions well into the modern era. While monarchy could be restored, as it was in 1660, the executed king could not be. With him had died some sense of the inevitability of kingly rule.

Originally written by contemporaries of King Charles's trial, the documents presented in the pages that follow help us understand the nature and significance of this event. Or, they will if read attentively: as with all such primary sources, they need to be examined with their authorship and intent in mind. One must ask who produced them, why, in what context, and for what purpose. Then, given the answers to these questions, one might judge what the sources can be trusted to tell us. The documents are, moreover, both sources and texts. As such, one might not only mine them for information about what happened but also consider how contemporaries read and reacted to the texts themselves, or at least how their authors might have hoped readers would interpret them. With such critical reading, these documents provide insight into the decisions to try the king, to execute him, and to abolish monarchy, and also into the ideas that shaped and grew from this momentous trial. To help in this task, the pages that follow begin with a brief introduction to contextualize the trial and the documents, a chronology of events, and a list of questions to consider.

Why did subjects of King Charles appoint themselves as his judges? Why did this man, once the most powerful person in three kingdoms, find himself on trial for his life in an English court? Born in Dunfermline, Scotland, in 1600, Charles was the second son of King James VI of Scotland and his wife, Anne of Denmark. In 1603, upon the death of Queen Elizabeth of England, her Scottish cousin James assumed the English crown as well, and with it the crown of Ireland. Scotland and England remained separate kingdoms—the union that formed Great Britain happened only in 1707—but James then wore the crowns of each, as his son after him would do. The short, shy, stammering younger sibling of a popular Prince of Wales, Charles only became heir to the crowns upon his brother's death from typhoid fever in 1612. He succeeded his father in 1625, inheriting with the crowns a number of problems to which he soon added. By 1642, Charles was at war with subjects in all three of his kingdoms. The problems that led to these wars might briefly be summed up as religious, financial, and constitutional, all complicated by the difficulties of a weak monarch trying to rule three distinct countries.[3]

---

3   The literature on the causes of the Civil Wars and the revolution(s) that took place around them is vast. A few classics and useful starting points on the wars and their causes include: John Morrill, *Stuart Britain: A Very Short Introduction* (Oxford: Oxford UP, 2000); Conrad Russell, *The Causes of the English Civil War* (Oxford: Oxford UP, 1990); Conrad Russell, *The Fall of the British Monarchies, 1637–1642* (Oxford: Oxford UP, 1991); David Cressy, *England on Edge: Crisis and Revolution, 1640–1642* (Oxford: Oxford UP, 2006); Ian Gentles, *The English Revolution and the Wars of the Three Kingdoms* (Harlow: Pearson Longman, 2007); and Michael Braddick, *God's Fury, England's Fire: A New History of the English Civil Wars* (London: Allen Lane, 2008).

The religious reformations of the sixteenth century had led to deep divisions, of differing sorts in all three realms. England had fitfully and finally become Protestant, abandoning its Catholic past. While some Catholics remained, "anti-popery"—a virulent suspicion of all things associated with the Catholic Pope—pervaded English culture by the early seventeenth century. The bulk of the country's Protestants may have shared this fear or disgust for Roman Catholicism, but they divided on other issues. One historian has memorably summed up the English church settlement under Queen Elizabeth as creating a church that "looked Catholic and sounded Protestant": while it embraced Protestant belief and doctrine, it retained some aspects of tradition, not least a system of church governance dominated by bishops.[4] Quite how much "compromise" the church ought to make with the past remained a heated point of contention. The "hotter sort of Protestants," sometimes called puritans, feared an episcopal hierarchy (that is, governance by bishops) as unbiblical and a source of the corruption they thought had rotted away the old church. Compounding the existing tensions, King Charles and his Archbishop of Canterbury began promoting within the church a group known as Arminians,[5] thought by their opponents to be bringing back more and more of the discarded Catholic past and thus to be endangering the souls of all. Meanwhile, the reformation in Ireland remained nominal, officially Protestant but with most people resolutely Catholic. The Scottish reformation, in contrast, had been the most "thorough" of the three: it had produced a Presbyterian church, Calvinist in doctrine like the English but initially without bishops. King James had reintroduced episcopacy in Scotland, a project Charles continued. Indeed, while a number of English Protestants hoped to see their church look more like that of the Scots, King Charles tried to make his Scottish church look more like that to the south. By 1639, groups of his Scottish subjects were at war with him. Called "Covenanters," they swore a solemn communal oath to oppose all innovations in religion that might endanger their salvation.

Charles also inherited a financially straitened kingdom. In England, royal revenues seemed never to keep up with the mounting costs of war and government. No longer able to live and run the country off the crown's own rents and revenues from its massive landed estates, Elizabeth and then James and Charles had to turn more often to taxation, and taxation required the consent of parliament. Consultative bodies convened at the king's command, parliaments included all the estates of the realm: in one house, lords secular and ecclesiastical—that is, noblemen and bishops—and in the other, representatives of the commons. Medieval parliaments had secured acknowledgements that kings ought only to collect taxes in extraordinary circumstances, and upon their approval. James and Charles after him turned more often to parliaments for taxes, and more often had to fight for the necessary consent. Some members of parliament (MPs) came to use their control of taxation as a way to secure royal attention to other grievances. Charles turned

---

4   Conrad Russell, "The Reformation and the Creation of the Church of England, 1500–1640," in *The Oxford Illustrated History of Tudor and Stuart Britain,* ed. John Morrill (Oxford: Oxford UP, 1996), 280.

5   Arminians taught that salvation was a work of both God and the believer, the product of grace and choice, a view thought by some to conflict with the English Church's accepted statement of doctrine.

to non-parliamentary sources of revenue, sometimes of dubious legality and enforced with measures of even more dubious legality. When respectable country gentlemen found themselves imprisoned without charge for refusing to pay a "forced loan," for example, and treated in ways usually reserved for seditious conspirators who threatened the security of the realm, financial problems quickly acquired constitutional implications. Charles's 1628 parliament presented him with a document known as the Petition of Right, recalling Magna Carta and insisting upon traditional liberties that must not be infringed, including freedom from imprisonment without cause shown, martial law, and non-parliamentary taxation. Fractious debates with parliament continued, however. After bringing the 1629 session to an abrupt end, Charles ruled the next eleven years on his own, without calling a parliament at all.

When Charles found himself at war with his Scottish subjects in 1639, he finally needed to call an English parliament to help gather the funds to fight. English members of parliament saw themselves with a chance to right some wrongs. The hasty dissolution of this so-called "Short Parliament" showed that Charles was not yet sufficiently desperate to bow. When the Scots invaded England and demanded that any terms of concord be ratified in an English parliament, though, another parliamentary session convened. This became known as the "Long Parliament." It would be the one to go to war against Charles. The situation need not necessarily have ended in war: initially MPs secured some concessions from the king, forcing him to abandon much of the judicial machinery and personnel that had allowed him to rule without parliament for the previous eleven years, but still grievances remained. When Irish Catholics rose in rebellion in 1641, alarmed that English and Scottish Protestants might join forces against them, this heightened both English MPs' fears and Charles's needs. By 1642, war began in England, too.

Not all MPs sided with the parliament in the English war; Charles had supporters. Nor did many, if any, people at the beginning of the conflict envision getting rid of the king. Rather, they wanted to tame him and to assert that parliament was a necessary, legitimate partner in governing. But a long, bloody series of brutal battles came to radicalize some. War ended briefly in 1646, with parliament victorious but Charles refusing its terms. A second set of battles erupted in 1648. Again, Charles lost. Soldiers within parliament's own "New Model Army" became increasingly disillusioned by their paymasters, fearing that too many MPs contemplated capitulating to the demands of a twice-defeated king, who had now shown himself to be a "man of blood," a man against whom God demanded vengeance, perfidious, untrustworthy, and determined to get his own way at whatever cost to his subjects' lives and livelihoods.[6] During the years of fighting, with greater freedom of movement than ever before and with traditional press censorship in tatters, new voices and new ideas made their way into public discourse. MPs had abandoned the episcopal church, replacing it with a presbyterian[7] model, but some people now argued against

---

6   Patricia Crawford, "Charles Stuart, That Man of Blood," *Journal of British Studies* 16.2 (1977): 41–61.

7   Church government on the Scottish model, by elected assemblies of elders, or "presbyters," rather than by bishops.

any one national church structure at all. A group known as the Levellers sought a new constitution for the country; they insisted that sovereignty lay with the people, not kings, calling for equality before the law and something akin to religious liberty. Others, more radical still, derided not just the kingly power but all its appendages, which included private property and clerical, legal, and educational monopolies of privilege. Some men insisted that whatever parliament's aims might have been, they had been fighting for freedoms of their own. Even some army leaders with little patience for ideas like those of the Levellers came to despair of ever bringing the king to terms. With some within its ranks calling for justice against a killer, and others at least desperate to bring the conflicts to a firm end, the army acted. On 6 December 1648, Colonel Pride and his men purged parliament of its moderate members, briefly arresting some and turning others away.

What was to happen thereafter? Some army leaders had long since determined that Charles must face trial, whether from providentialist notions that God demanded vengeance upon him, some mix of republican thinking derived from both classical and biblical texts, or convictions of popular sovereignty based on custom and experience.[8] A lieutenant-general and second in command of the New Model Army, Oliver Cromwell—"at least *a* and probably *the* driving force" pushing for the king's trial—seems initially to have wanted the king's deposition in favour of one of his sons and came to regicide only reluctantly. Cromwell, like others, had struggled to discern "what the mind of God may be in all this, and what our duty is."[9] Such doubts and differences meant that the purged parliament only passed the measure creating a High Court of Justice for the king's trial on 6 January 1649, and only after the Commons decided to ignore the recalcitrant residuum of the House of Lords. The court began its discussions two days later, meeting in the venue where traditionally the king's own courts sat. Two stalwart, respected lawyers assumed key duties: John Bradshaw as the court's president, John Cooke as chief prosecutor. On 20 January, the king himself appeared to face his judges and the charge of treason, murder, and other high crimes against the people of England. He refused, however, to enter a plea and thus to recognize the legitimacy of the court. Repeatedly, his judges urged him to plead; repeatedly, he did not deign to do so. Normally, an individual refusing to enter a plea would have been literally pressed to do so: crushed under heavy weights until death or compliance. In Charles's case, finally, on 27 January the judges deemed him guilty. Three days later, Charles faced a masked executioner on a scaffold outside his Banqueting House at Whitehall. The gathered crowd watched as he, like so many criminals before him, was killed in the name of law and justice.

Unlike the many others executed as criminals in these years, however, Charles Stuart had been an anointed king. Even after years of brutal civil war had tarnished the significance of that status, the shock of his killing ran deep. The distress and novelty can

---

8   On the role of republicanism in these developments, see in particular Sarah Barber, *Regicide and Republicanism: Politics and Ethics in the English Revolution, 1646–1659* (Edinburgh: Edinburgh UP, 1998).

9   John Morrill and Philip Baker, "Oliver Cromwell, the Regicide, and the Sons of Zeruiah," in *The Regicides and the Execution of Charles I*, ed. Jason Peacey (Basingstoke: Palgrave Macmillan), 14–35, quotes at 15 and 27.

be overstated, however: two anointed queens had, after all, been executed on English soil in the not too distant past, both Anne Boleyn for (supposedly) committing treason against her husband, King Henry VIII, and Charles's grandmother, Mary Queen of Scots, after her own subjects had deposed her and she became embroiled in plots against Queen Elizabeth.[10] The latter execution, in particular, proved a particularly fraught precedent: subjects of Queen Elizabeth had insisted that she was a public person, with duties to the public and a "state" somewhat separable from the person wearing the crown, and as such, had to execute her sister queen whatever her private preferences.[11] In two senses, then, that execution had shown the way to this one. The notion that parliament might legitimately depose a king, too, had been voiced before.[12] Even so, this *was* new. Even more emphatically novel was the decision to kill off the monarchy along with the king.

Precisely how matters came to this point, and why, remain subjects of debate amongst historians. In his foundational study of these events, S.R. Gardiner pointed to the long delay between the purging of parliament on 6 December and the onset of the trial in late January, arguing that army leaders and their civilian allies tried in these weeks to secure their own settlement with the king. Only from late December or early January did the trial and execution become set.[13] In her classic narrative of the trial, Veronica Wedgwood treated its conclusion as essentially fixed from at least the moment soldiers seized Charles from parliamentary control and purged the Commons, if not sooner. The end took nearly two months to arrive because the men behind the trial needed time to make it appear legal and legitimate.[14] Sean Kelsey, in contrast, has argued that the trial's outcome was far from foreordained, presenting the trial itself as one more attempt at negotiation. He observes that some in the army warned against killing the king as they thought it a tactical error; they had this king in their physical control, but upon his death, his son would immediately be proclaimed king in his stead and be free of their hands. While some people had certainly come to think it necessary that Charles die, others thought him even more dangerous dead than alive. Kelsey argues, then, that even as the trial began, its judges had not decided upon death; they hoped to use it to compel concessions from the king, beginning most crucially with a recognition of their

---

10 Two other women recognized as queens had also been executed—Queen Katherine Howard and Queen Jane—though neither had been anointed at coronations.

11 For an overview, see K.J. Kesselring, "Mary Queen of Scots and the Northern Rebellion of 1569," in *Leadership in Elizabethan England*, ed. Peter Iver Kaufman (Basingstoke: Palgrave Macmillan, 2012), 51–72, and "License to Kill: Assassination and the Politics of Murder in Elizabethan and Early Stuart England," *Canadian Journal of History* 48 (2013): 421–40.

12 William Harrison's description of parliament in his contribution to Holinshed's *Chronicles* had made this point explicitly; see Annabel Patterson, *Reading Holinshed's Chronicles* (Chicago: U of Chicago P, 1994), 103–04. On sixteenth-century formulations of tyrannicidal thought, see too Roger Mason and Martin S. Smith, *A Dialogue on the Law of Kingship among the Scots: A Critical Edition and Translation of George Buchanan's De Iure Regni apud Scotos Dialogus* (Aldershot: Ashgate, 2004).

13 S.R. Gardiner, *History of the Great Civil War, 1642–1649* (London, 1893, 4 vols.), IV, 283–88.

14 C.V. Wedgwood, *A King Condemned: The Trial and Execution of Charles I*, 2nd ed. (London: I.B. Tauris, 2011). On these fraught few weeks, see, too, David Underdown, *Pride's Purge* (Oxford: Oxford UP, 1971).

authority and thus that of "the people." They gave him chance after chance to enter a plea, but Charles overplayed a strong hand and forced them finally to find him guilty and order his execution.[15]

Kelsey reminds us of the dangers of a teleological misreading of developments based on our knowledge of the ending. He valuably highlights the contingency and lack of unanimity in events, but somewhat overstates the case. Clive Holmes, in contrast, points to those MPs and commissioners of the court who left London as the trial began, convinced that no further compromise might happen and refusing to involve themselves in the king's death. Holmes argues that Kelsey chose and read his evidence poorly, erring in trusting accounts by royalists that were based on wishful thinking or hearsay, for example, and suggests that Kelsey pushed even accurate readings too far by using the sentiments of a few to characterize a majority. Holmes draws on evidence from the trials of the king's judges, as they would themselves be called to account when the wheel of fortune turned and monarchy was restored in 1660. He quotes the plaintive words of John Downes, one of the signatories to the king's death warrant, who maintained that he had wanted to save Charles throughout the trial but could not: "I did my best; I could do no more: I was single; I was alone."[16]

Historians have differed, too, in how they characterize the king's trial and its outcome, based in part on their own politics as well as prevailing narratives about English (or British) history. Was the king's execution a tragedy wrought by desperation or a few aberrant men? A crime of the worst magnitude? A regrettable necessity? A laudable challenge to either (or both) an individual autocratic ruler or a political system of manifest inequality? As the saying goes, "history is written by the victors": generations of British historians writing in the aftermath of monarchy's restoration tended to see these events as tragic.[17] Recently, however, Geoffrey Robertson, a prominent human rights lawyer, has depicted the trial as a vital precedent for modern efforts to try war criminals and political leaders responsible for crimes against humanity. Against those who deride the trial as a legal monstrosity, he lauds the solicitor who prosecuted the case, John Cooke, as a trailblazing proponent of legal protections we now hold dear and as a defender of the rule of law.[18] Ann Hughes, a respected historian of the era, has argued that depictions of the execution as "an unnatural mistake" driven only by rogues and religious fanatics are misleading, derived from a "comforting, moderate mythology of English history that the English do not do this sort of thing."[19]

---

15   Sean Kelsey, "Staging the Trial of Charles I," in *The Regicides and the Execution of Charles I*, 71–93; "The Trial of Charles I," *English Historical Review* 118 (2003): 585–616; "The Death of Charles I," *Historical Journal* 45 (2002): 727–54; and "Politics and Procedure in the Trial of Charles I," *Law and History Review* 22 (2004): 1–25.

16   Clive Holmes, "The Trial and Execution of Charles I," *Historical Journal* 53 (2010): 289–310, quote at 304.

17   A good overview of the historiography can be found in Jason Peacey's introduction to *The Regicides and the Execution of Charles I*, 1–13.

18   Geoffrey Robertson, *The Tyrannicide Brief: The Story of the Man Who Sent Charles I to the Scaffold* (London: Chatto & Windus, 2005).

19   Ann Hughes, "The Execution of Charles I," www.bbc.co.uk/history/british/civil_war_revolution/charlesi_execution_01.shtml

In such disagreements, historians sometimes echo the differing interpretations of contemporaries. Those involved in these events sought desperately to shape how people in their own day would understand and respond to them. Members of the Rump Parliament[20] and the High Court of Justice arranged both to have a "perfect record" of the trial filed with the clerk of parliament and to have journalists on hand to report it to the public at large. Precursors to the modern newspaper, newsbooks conveyed varying accounts of these events to contemporary audiences, all with their own particular spin.[21] Causing particular damage to parliament's portrayal of its actions, though, was a work published immediately after the execution and in multiple editions thereafter, ostensibly (but not really) written by the king and depicting him as a Christ-like martyr: *Eikon Basilike, The Portraiture of His Sacred Majesty in His Solitudes and Sufferings*.[22] The great poet John Milton prepared potent defences of the regicide and republic, in both English and Latin, for audiences domestic and international.[23] The republic and the government of Oliver Cromwell that followed ultimately proved unstable, however, which ensured the triumph of interpretations favourable to the monarchy as restored in 1660—though never to the exclusion of all other reactions and remembrances. Huge and happy crowds greeted the triumphal entry of King Charles II into London in 1660; but even so, the courts kept busy prosecuting individuals who dared voice their dissent.[24] When the new king sought vengeance against the men responsible for his father's death, many applauded, but not all.

The documents that follow fall into three sections: first, accounts of the king's trial, then short selections from a range of texts that give some sense of the variety of responses the trial and execution engendered, and finally an account of the trial of Major-General Thomas Harrison, one of the so-called "regicides," the men held most responsible for

---

20 The name given to the remnant of the parliament that remained after the army purged it on 6 December 1648 of members who still wished to negotiate with the king.

21 For news culture in these years, see especially works by Jason Peacey, including his essay on "Reporting a Revolution: A Failed Propaganda Campaign," in *The Regicides and the Execution of Charles I*, 161–80 and *Print and Public Politics in the English Revolution* (Cambridge: Cambridge UP, 2013).

22 For a good, accessible modern edition and useful discussion, see Jim Daems and Holly Faith Nelson, ed., *Eikon Basilike with Selections from Eikonoklastes* (Peterborough: Broadview, 2005). For an extremely useful set of essays touching on this and many other features of these years, including how news of the events spread throughout the British Atlantic world and how people of various sorts responded in a wide variety of texts, see Laura Lunger Knoppers, ed., *The Oxford Handbook of Literature and the English Revolution* (Oxford: Oxford UP, 2012).

23 John Milton, *The Tenure of Kings and Magistrates* (1649); *Eikonoklastes* (1649); *Defensio pro populo Anglicano* (1652); and *Defensio secunda* (1654). On Milton in this context, see in particular Laura Lunger Knoppers, *Historicizing Milton: Spectacle, Power and Poetry in Restoration England* (Athens: U of Georgia P, 1994).

24 On the range of reactions to the restoration of monarchy, see for example, Tim Harris, *Restoration: Charles II and His Kingdoms, 1660–1685* (London: Allen Lane, 2006), 48–56, and J.C. Jeaffreson, ed., *Middlesex County Records*, ed. (London, 1888), vol. III, 303–06, including the indictment of Margret Osmond for saying that the "King's Majesty [who] is dead was lawfully put to death" and that "Charles the Second shall not reign one year."

the death of Charles I.[25] The testimony reproduced in this work adds detail to the main account of the king's trial, conveying something of the motives of the king's judges and the horror of the king's supporters, while also providing an instructive contrast to the king's trial.

The key text to include is, of course, an account of Charles's encounter with the High Court of Justice. Several contemporary reports of Charles's trial exist, all of which differ in some respects. Two "official" manuscript accounts survive, drawn up by clerks of the High Court, likely in response to an order by the Commons in early February of 1649 that a record of the proceedings be prepared for posterity: one is now in the State Papers collection at the National Archives while the other, a roll prepared by court clerk John Phelps, is now kept in the Parliamentary Archives.[26] Phelps himself was specially exempted from the Act of Oblivion and Indemnity that accompanied the restoration of monarchy in 1660 and had to flee for safety to the Continent, dying a few years later in Switzerland.[27] His roll formed the basis of a royalist publication on the trial in 1684: perhaps prompted by a plot against Charles II in 1683, John Nalson published the official record, along with some additions and a fervidly royalist preface of his own, as *A True Copy of the Journal of the High Court of Justice for the Tryal of K. Charles I*, attempting to darken the memory of the regicides by using their own words against them. Nearer the time of the trial itself, a number of journalists reported it in print, including two who received special access and the Court's permission to publish their accounts of the event as it unfolded. Henry Walker issued *Collections of Notes Taken at the King's Tryall* in several installments, along with notes in his weekly newsbook, *Perfect Occurrences*. Gilbert Mabbott published first *A Perfect Narrative of the Whole Proceedings of the High Court of Justice*, then two editions of

---

25 Surprisingly little scholarly work has been done on the regicides and their trials, but a few good studies do exist. See in particular Howard Nenner, "Trial of the Regicides: Retribution and Treason in 1660," in *Politics and the Political Imagination in Late Stuart Britain*, ed. Howard Nenner (Woodbridge: Boydell and Brewer, 1998), 21–42 and Knoppers, *Historicizing Milton*, 42–66. Melinda Zook also has an essay on the trials of the regicides forthcoming in *Rethinking the State Trials*, ed. Brian Cowan and Scott Sowerby (Woodbridge: Boydell and Brewer). A recent popular history follows those who got away, not least the three who ended up in New England: Don Jordan and Michael Walsh, *The King's Revenge: Charles II and the Greatest Manhunt in British History* (London: Little, Brown, 2012). An accessible and immensely useful set of primary sources by one of the regicides who escaped offers an excellent starting point: *The Memoirs of Edmund Ludlow, Lieutenant-General of the Horse in the Army of the Commonwealth of England, 1625–1672*, ed. C.H. Firth (Oxford, 1894, 2 vols.).

26 The National Archives, Kew, SP 16/517; the Parliamentary Archives, London, HL/PO/JO/10/14/11A. For discussion of these two manuscripts, see M.F. Bond, ed., *Manuscripts of the House of Lords, Addenda, 1514–1714* (London: HMSO, 1962), xviii–xix. J.G. Muddiman reproduced the first, with some errors and additions, in his staunchly royalist *Trial of King Charles the First* (Edinburgh, 1928). John Rushworth's description of the trial and execution has also been widely cited. Secretary in turn to Thomas Fairfax and Oliver Cromwell and then to one of the men who would lead the trials of the regicides, Rushworth had privileged access to many papers. Yet, the volume of his *Historical Collections* that covers the trial was published only in 1690 and seems to draw heavily on contemporary printed accounts. Roger Lockyer edited an edition of it for the Folio Society in 1959: *The Trial of King Charles the First* (London: Folio Society, 1959). The nineteenth-century *State Trials*, ed. T. Howell, combines bits from Mabbott, Nalson, and others. *The Trial of Charles I: A Documentary History*, ed. David Lagomarsino and Charles J. Wood (Hanover: UP of New England, 1989) compiles brief selections from Mabbott, Nalson, Rushworth and a few other contemporaries to produce a coherent account, though at the expense of clarity about the origin or nature of those sources.

27 C.H. Firth, "Phelps, John (b. 1618/19)," rev. Timothy Venning, *Oxford Dictionary of National Biography* (Oxford, 2004; online ed. 2008).

A Continuation of the Narrative, all brought together in February of 1649 under the title *King Charls His Tryal*. Jason Peacey, an historian specializing in the press and propaganda of these years, notes that royalists at the time did not challenge the accuracy of these journalists' accounts, and indeed, republished Mabbott's work in later years, with new titles and prefaces, in their own attempts to brand the proceedings a "black tribunal."[28]

Given constraints on space (and the time and patience of readers), only one of these trial accounts can be included here. I have opted to use Nalson's 1684 edition of Phelps's parliament roll, marked with asterisks, italics, and explanatory notes to indicate where Nalson added to or diverged from his source. The journalists' publications at the time of the trial would have shaped many contemporaries' understanding of events and might thus be preferable; but Phelps's record (and thus Nalson's work, too) includes more of the scene-setting elements and the testimony of witnesses heard in private sessions of the Court that were not ultimately revealed in the public parts of the trial or in the journalists' accounts. Nalson also introduces passages from Mabbott's reports when he thinks they add useful detail, and paraphrases from a government-authorized account of the king's speech from the scaffold. His royalist interjections into texts prepared by and for those who brought the king to trial also make his version particularly interesting.

When reading the trial accounts included here, keeping in mind their value as both sources and texts, one further bit of context might also be usefully considered: trial reporting as practice and genre. Over the eighteenth and nineteenth centuries, publishers produced vast collections of so-called "state trial" accounts, describing them as edifying as well as entertaining. Editors of these collections generally wrote of their desire to educate by example and to cultivate an informed and engaged citizenry.[29] The collections and the individual accounts often emerged from partisan motives, too. As such, it should perhaps not surprise us to learn that trial reporting only really took shape in the sixteenth century, both because the spread of printing technology made it possible and because the emergence of oppositional voices into nascent public spheres of political discourse made it desirable.[30] Annabel Patterson briefly traces this history in her edition of the trial of Nicholas Throckmorton. A Protestant opponent of the Catholic Queen

---

28 See Peacey, "Failed Campaign" and, for an example of a royalist republication of one of these works, *Englands Black Tribunall* (London, 1660). On Mabbott, see, too, Patrick Keola Marchard Ludolph, "'Fitt for Many Imployments': Gilbert Mabbott, the London Press, and the Working of Westminster" (PhD dissertation, University of California, Santa Barbara, 2014). My thanks to the author for sharing with me a copy of this dissertation.

29 For a discussion of the development of the "state trials" collections in the eighteenth century, see Brian Cowan, ed., *The State Trial of Doctor Henry Sacheverell* (London: Wiley-Blackwell, 2012), esp. 30–34.

30 One might also consider how accurate an account of someone's words might have been, with even the best of intentions from the reporter, given that shorthand writing techniques only seemed to become well known from the early seventeenth century, with the publication of works such as Thomas Shelton's *Short Writing* (London, 1626). This problem is alluded to in a 1681 edition of a manuscript account of the 1586 trial of Mary Queen of Scots and other plotters against Queen Elizabeth. The person publishing these trial accounts defended their authenticity, but noted, "tis confessed, the same are not so exactly taken as the trials of the present age, the ingenious skill of speedy and short writing being much improved since those times." M.D., *A Brief History of the Life of Mary, Queen of Scots... with a full account of the tryals of that Queen* (London, 1681), 1.

Mary, Throckmorton survived a trial for treason in 1554, an account of which an anonymous author subsequently prepared for publication. Patterson suggests that this trial proved influential as a model of how and why trial transcripts should be made public.[31] Summarized accounts of the trial of Sir Thomas More in 1534 had illegally made their way into print, produced by people who sympathized with More in his conflict with King Henry VIII.[32] The reporter of Throckmorton's trial used a dramatized dialogue form, purporting to offer readers a transcript of what participants said in the court, again from oppositional motives. John Foxe included ostensible trial transcripts and accounts to great emotional effect in his influential history of the nascent Protestant church, best known as the *Book of Martyrs*. Under Queen Elizabeth, officials came to see the value in presenting their own accounts of important trials, to help shape public interpretation. Certainly, courts had previously produced records, but rarely verbatim accounts, and never made them public. Indeed, royal officials filed the records of important trials separately from regular court papers in something called the "baga de secretis," locked away in a special cabinet.[33] The publication of any trial account, then, had its own particular motives and conventions and cannot be seen as a neutral act. However disingenuously, such accounts call upon readers to judge for themselves.

Finally, my own editorial interventions should be kept in mind. This is a classroom edition, not a scholarly one, intended to make these texts more accessible. As such, I have modernized spelling and punctuation: I have, for example, normalized v/u, i/j, and the use of "y" to indicate "th," standardized the spelling of place names to their commonly accepted current forms, cut up long sentences to improve clarity, and updated older verb forms ending in –th. I have silently expanded some abbreviations and cut some redundant phrasing (e.g, "he this deponent" gets shortened to "he"). Square brackets indicate any additions or omissions, as well as some clarifications. I have modernized capitalization, too, keeping it to a minimum but at some cost: Some of these authors capitalized the first letter of all words pertaining to the king as one might capitalize words relating to a divinity and they also tended to capitalize words for important concepts such as "the People," "Justice," and "Law." Rightly or wrongly, these capitals have gone. I have retained "old style" dating but treated the new year as beginning on January 1: While most Catholic countries adopted the modern Gregorian, or Western, calendar in 1582, the English only did so in 1752, leaving their dates ten (eventually eleven) days

---

31 Annabel Patterson, ed., *The Trial of Nicholas Throckmorton* (Toronto: Centre for Reformation and Renaissance Studies, 1998); see also her discussion in *Reading Holinshed's Chronicles*, 154–83. For a recent call to think critically, in both literary and historical ways, about the truth claims in depositions, published works claiming to be "True Relations," and other such texts of the period, see Frances Dolan, *True Relations: Reading, Literature and Evidence in Seventeenth-Century England* (Philadelphia: U of Pennsylvania P, 2013). Cynthia Herrup, too, approaches trial accounts as a genre with a history in *A House in Gross Disorder: Sex, Law and the 2nd Earl of Castlehaven* (Oxford: Oxford UP, 1999).

32 See Duncan Derrett, "Neglected Versions of the Contemporary Account of the Trial of Sir Thomas More," *Bulletin of the Institute of Historical Research* 33 (1960): 202–23.

33 See L.W. Vernon Harcourt, "The Baga de Secretis," *English Historical Review* 23 (1908): 508–29.

behind those using the "new style" calendar. They also dated the new year as beginning on March 25. In line with standard historical practice, I have kept the first but updated the second. Thus, where these English authors wrote the date of King Charles's execution as 30 January 1648, and a Continental writer might have written it as 9 February 1649, it is given here as 30 January 1649.

CHRONOLOGY

1600   Charles is born in Scotland.

1603   Charles's father, King James VI of Scotland, becomes King James I of England and of Ireland upon the death of Queen Elizabeth.

1606   Thomas Harrison, future major-general and regicide, is born.

1618   The Thirty Years' War begins on the continent.

1625   Charles becomes king of England, Scotland, and Ireland upon the death of his father.

Charles marries the French Catholic Princess Henrietta Maria, daughter of King Henry IV (assassinated in 1610) and sister of King Louis XIII.

1628   The English parliament presents Charles with the Petition of Right, the product of disputes over taxes not approved by parliament, billeting of soldiers, martial law, and other actions its members deemed infringements of English liberties.

Charles's friend and advisor, the unpopular Duke of Buckingham, is assassinated.

1629   Charles dissolves an English parliament that criticized his taxes and religious policies, beginning what in retrospect became known as "the personal rule," with no parliament called for eleven years.

1637   Charles introduces into Presbyterian Scotland a variant of the English Book of Common Prayer, provoking widespread dissent that coheres into the Covenanter movement.

1639   The First Bishops' War, between Charles and his rebellious Scottish subjects, the opening salvo in what will become the "Wars of the Three Kingdoms."

1640   The Second Bishops' War; Scottish Covenanters occupy northern England; Charles is forced to call an English parliament to secure funds.

England's "Short Parliament" meets, April–May.

England's "Long Parliament" begins meeting in November.

1641   Members of the Long Parliament abolish the Courts of Star Chamber and High Commission and put on trial the Earl of Strafford, one of the king's confidants, moving against the instruments and personnel that had enabled Charles's "personal rule."

Irish Rebellion begins, October.

1642   English Civil War formally begins when Charles raises his standard at Nottingham, 22 August.

Battle of Edgehill, first pitched battle of the war, 23 October.

1644 Battle of Marston Moor: combined forces of English Parliamentarians and Scottish Covenanters defeat Royalists, 2 July.

1645 Book of Common Prayer replaced by a new Directory of Public Worship; Archbishop Laud executed.

Parliament creates its New Model Army, bringing together separate regional armies under centralized command.

Battle of Naseby, 14 June: a decisive defeat of Royalist forces by the parliamentary army under the command of Sir Thomas Fairfax and Oliver Cromwell; beginning of the end of the First English Civil War.

1646 Charles surrenders to a Scottish army, 5 May. Remaining Royalist garrisons surrender over the coming months.

Episcopacy formally abolished, October.

1647 Scottish army leaves England and hands Charles to the English parliament.

English parliament threatens to disband the New Model Army; Cornet Joyce and his soldiers seize Charles from parliamentary control, 4 June.

New Model Army marches into London, 6 August.

Putney Debates, October: Levellers and radical soldiers argue that they are fighting for rights beyond those envisioned by parliamentary leaders.

Charles escapes to the Isle of Wight and is again under parliamentary control, November; peace negotiations continue with various parties; in December, he makes a secret "engagement" with a Scottish faction that comes to be known as the Engagers.

1648 Second English Civil War begins; the Battle of Preston in August marks the beginning of its end, with the New Model Army defeating Royalists and their Scottish Engager allies.

Treaty of Newport, September: failed attempt to negotiate a peace between parliament and King Charles.

Treaty of Westphalia, October: end of the Thirty Years' War on the continent.

Army's Remonstrance, November: showing Leveller influence, the army demands an end to the negotiations and that Charles be brought to justice.

Pride's Purge, 6 December: Colonel Thomas Pride and his soldiers purge parliament of those members deemed to be enemies of the army for their willingness to compromise with the defeated king, leaving only some 80 members in what became known as the Rump Parliament.

Army council orders that Charles be brought to Windsor, 16 December.

House of Commons introduces an Ordinance for the trial of the king, 23 December.

1649 House of Commons passes the Ordinance, now declared to be an Act of Parliament although the Lords rejected it, 6 January.

Judges of the newly created High Court of Justice convene in the Painted Chamber of the Palace of Westminster, 8 January.

John Bradshaw named as president of the High Court, 10 January.

Charles's trial begins, 20 January.

Charles's death warrant is signed, 27–29 January.

Charles is executed, 30 January.

Eikon Basilike, purportedly by Charles I, appears in print.

The Scottish parliament declares the eldest son of Charles I to be King Charles II, 5 February; a group of Irish Royalists also proclaim him as king.

Act Abolishing the Office of King is passed in England, 17 March.

Act Abolishing the House of Lords is passed, 19 March.

Act declaring England to be a Commonwealth is passed, 19 May.

Oliver Cromwell's campaign to defeat Irish rebels and Royalists begins, August.

1650 Oliver Cromwell becomes Lord General of the army after resignation of Fairfax, June.

Cromwell and his soldiers defeat the Scots, 3 September.

1651 Cromwell and his army defeat Charles II at Worcester, 3 September; he escapes to the continent.

1653 Cromwell dissolves the Rump Parliament, April.

The Instrument of Government makes Cromwell Lord Protector, December.

1655 Cromwell appoints major-generals to govern the counties, September.

1658 Oliver Cromwell dies, 3 September; his son Richard becomes Lord Protector.

1659 The army dissolves the Protectorate Parliament in April; Richard Cromwell resigns and the Rump reconvenes in May; army replaces the Rump in October, but it returns on 26 December.

1660 General George Monck marches his forces south from Scotland in January; under his direction, members of the Long Parliament excluded at Pride's Purge reconvene in February and then dissolve the parliament to hold new elections.

Convention Parliament opens in April.

Charles II issues conciliatory Declaration of Breda on 1 May, promising that punishment of malefactors in the wars will be left to parliament's determination.

Charles II proclaimed as king of England, 8 May; enters London on 29 May.

Act of Free and General Pardon, Indemnity and Oblivion, debated since May, passes on 29 August, excepting in particular those involved in the trial and execution of Charles I.

1660
(continued)

Trial of the regicides begins, 10 October.

Trial and conviction of Major-General Thomas Harrison, 11 October.

Harrison's execution, 13 October.

Trials and convictions of other regicides, 12–16 October. Executions on 15 October (John Carew), 16 (John Cooke and Hugh Peters), 17 (Thomas Scot, Gregory Clement, Adrian Scroop, and John Jones), and 19 (Daniel Axtell and Francis Hacker).

1661

Bodies of Oliver Cromwell, John Bradshaw, and Henry Ireton exhumed and "executed," 30 January.

1662

Executions of three more regicides: Miles Corbet, John Okey, and John Barkstead, captured in the Netherlands, executed in England on 19 April. Henry Vane, not a signatory of Charles's death warrant but a staunch republican (and former governor of Massachusetts), was also condemned for treason in this round up and executed on 14 June.

The newly revised and reissued Book of Common Prayer includes special prayers to mark each 30 January as a day to commemorate "Charles the Martyr" for his defence of the church and to give thanks for the kingdom's deliverance. A cult of the Royal Martyr grows; prayers for Charles the Martyr persist in Prayer Book revisions until 1859.

QUESTIONS TO CONSIDER

1. Why try the king? Why did King Charles's opponents decide upon a trial?

2. Did the trial indict the institution of monarchy itself, or did it indict Charles for being a bad monarch?

3. What arguments and evidence did the king's opponents use to support their claim that kings were bound by law and that sovereignty rested in the people, not in kings? What role did arguments grounded in history play in their case? What of arguments grounded in religious belief and the Bible?

4. What might explain Charles's intransigence at his trial? Why not answer the charge and try to defend himself? What might explain the Court's decision to allow him so many opportunities to enter a plea?

5. At Charles's trial, was a guilty verdict inevitable? Was a death sentence? Was the abolition of monarchy thereafter inevitable?

6. What was the relationship between regicide and republicanism? Does one necessarily imply the other?

7. Why did the High Court judges have Charles's trial reported? What does that decision suggest about the motives of those responsible for holding the trial? Why would royalists in turn republish the same accounts?

8. Is the term "regicide" problematic? Why or why not? Why might some of those who defended Charles's execution have denied the label?

9. What ceremonial aspects were introduced to the trial? Why, do you suppose?

10. In what ways might trials themselves be considered rituals?

11. In what ways were the trials of King Charles and Major-General Harrison alike and in what ways did they differ? In what ways were the performances of the two defendants alike?

12. Both Charles and Harrison identified themselves—and were identified by others—as martyrs. How so, and why?

13. What role did vengeance play in both the trial of the king and the trial of the regicides? Is vengeance antithetical to—or a fundamental constituent of—law or justice?

14. How does the definition of kingship as an office presented in Harrison's trial differ from that presented in the trial of King Charles?

15. How is treason defined in each trial?

16. Given that 59 men signed Charles I's death warrant—and that others were deeply involved in the trial as well—why were 10 men executed as regicides (and another 19 imprisoned for life) after monarchy was restored in 1660? Why execute any of them at that point? Or, why not execute more of them?

17. Do we get a sense anywhere in these documents of "the state" becoming depersonalized, separate or separable from the person of the king? Where, in contrast, do we get a sense of the state still being seen as the king's personal "estate"?

PART 1

Trying the King

DOCUMENT I:

From John Nalson, *A True Copy of the Journal of the High Court of Justice for the Tryal of K. Charles I, as it was Read in the House of Commons, and Attested under the hand of Phelps, Clerk to that Infamous Court* (London, 1684)

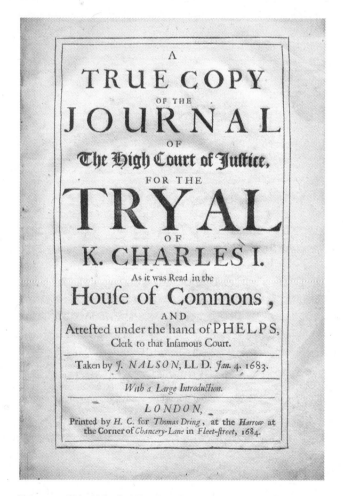

Title page of John Nalson's *A True Copy of the Journal of the High Court of Justice*, as published in 1684. Courtesy of Special Collections, Killam Library, Dalhousie University.

Born in 1637, John Nalson was only 12 years old when the High Court tried King Charles. In later life, he became an Anglican cleric and active polemicist, writing frequently to denounce both "papists" and "Commonwealth Protestants" (e.g., Presbyterians) as he thought them dangerous to the order and stability of a restored monarchy, House of Lords, and Anglican church. As one of his contributions to public discourse, he published this so-called "True Copy" of the official record of King Charles I's trial, dedicating the work to Charles's second son, James, brother of King Charles II and himself the future King James II/VII. Nalson opens the work with a lengthy, staunchly royalist introduction (omitted here) and also injects passages taken from journalist Gilbert Mabbott's contemporary reports on the trial and from an anonymous, government-authorized account of the king's scaffold speech, as well as a number of personal additions. These interpolations are indicated below, though readers now (as then) may well be able to spot them without assistance. This is, in a sense, a work with multiple authors and multiple purposes, something to consider as you read through the extracts.

❧

A Journal of the Proceedings of the High Court of Justice, erected By Act of the Commons of England, entitled, An Act of the Commons of England, Assembled in Parliament, for Erecting of a High Court of Justice, for the Trying and Judging of Charles Stuart, King of England. The tenor whereof follows, viz.

Whereas it is notorious, that Charles Stuart, the now king of England, not content with those many encroachments which his predecessors had made upon the people in their rights and freedoms, has had a wicked design totally to subvert the ancient and fundamental laws and liberties of this nation, and in their place to introduce an arbitrary and tyrannical government, and that besides all other evil ways and means to bring this design to pass, he has prosecuted it with fire and sword, levied and maintained a cruel war in the land, against the parliament and kingdom, whereby the country has been miserably wasted, the public treasure exhausted, trade decayed, thousands of people murdered, and infinite other mischiefs committed. For all which high and treasonable offences, the said Charles Stuart might long since justly have been brought to exemplary and **condign** punishment. Whereas also, the parliament well hoping that the restraint and imprisonment of his person, after it had pleased God to deliver him into their hands, would have quieted the distempers of the kingdom, did forbear to proceed judicially against him; but found by sad experience, that such their remissness served only to encourage him and his accomplices in the continuance of their evil practices, and in raising of new commotions, rebellions, and invasions; for prevention therefore of the like or greater inconveniences, and to the end no chief officer

condign: Worthy, appropriate, or deserved.

or magistrate whatsoever may hereafter presume traitorously and maliciously to imagine or contrive the enslaving or destroying of the English nation and to expect impunity for so doing, be it ordained and enacted by the Commons in parliament, and it is hereby ordained and enacted by authority thereof, that Thomas Lord **Fairfax**, Oliver **Cromwell**, Henry **Ireton**, esquires, Sir Hardress Waller, Philip Skippon, Valentine Wauton, Thomas Harrison [*and another 128 names listed, omitted here*] shall be and are hereby appointed and required to be commissioners and judges, for the hearing, trying and adjudging of the said Charles Stuart. And the said commissioners or any twenty or more of them, shall be and are hereby authorized and constituted a High Court of Justice to meet and sit at such convenient time and place as by the said commissioners or the major part of twenty or more of them under their hands and seals shall be appointed and notified by public proclamation in the great hall or Palace Yard at **Westminster**, and to adjourn from time to time, and from place to place, as the said High Court or major part thereof meeting shall hold fit; and to take order for the charging of him the said Charles Stuart with the crimes and treasons above mentioned; and for the receiving of his personal answer thereunto, and for the examination of witnesses upon oath, which the Court has hereby authority to administer, or otherwise, and taking any other evidence concerning the same, and thereupon, or in default of such answer, to proceed to final sentence according to justice and the merit of the cause, and such final sentence to execute or cause to be executed speedily and impartially. And the said Court is hereby authorized and required to appoint and direct all such officers, attendants, and other circumstances as they or the major part of them shall in any sort judge necessary or useful for the orderly and good managing of the premises. And Thomas Lord Fairfax the general, and all officers and soldiers under his command, and all officers of justice, and other well affected persons are hereby authorized and required to be aiding and assisting unto the said Court in the due execution of the trust hereby committed. Provided, that this Act, and the authority hereby granted, do continue in force for the space of one month from the making hereof, and no longer.

In pursuance of which said Act, the House of Commons ordered as follows, *viz.* [namely] Saturday, 6 January 1649:

Ordered by the Commons assembled in parliament, that the commissioners nominated in the Act for erecting of a High Court of Justice for the trying and judging of Charles Stuart, king of England, do meet on Monday next, at two o'clock in the afternoon, in the **Painted Chamber**.

By virtue of which said recited Act, and of the said order grounded thereupon, the commissioners whose names are here under-written [*list omitted here*], met on Monday, the said 8 January 1649, in the said Painted Chamber at Westminster, where the said Act was openly read and the Court called.

Fairfax (1612–71): Commander-in-chief of the New Model Army.

Cromwell (1599–1658): MP and, at this point, second in command of the New Model Army; later became Lord Protector of the Commonwealth of England, Scotland, and Ireland (1653–58).

Ireton (1611–51): MP, army general, and from 1646, Cromwell's son-in-law.

Westminster: Palace of Westminster, where parliaments and the royal courts met. Of the buildings, only Westminster Hall survived the fire of 1834.

Painted Chamber: Another room in the old Palace of Westminster, used for conferences between the Lords and Commons.

The commissioners of the Court being as aforesaid met and informing themselves of the tenor of their commission, they accordingly appoint the said Court to be held in the same place, on Wednesday, 10 January, and ordered proclamation thereof to be made in the great hall at Westminster, by Edward Dendy, sergeant at arms, authorizing him thereunto by precept under their hands and seals, in these words following, *viz.*

By virtue of an Act of the Commons of England assembled in parliament for erecting of an High Court of Justice for the trying and judging of Charles Stuart, king of England, we whose names are hereunder written (being commissioners, amongst others nominated in the said Act) do hereby appoint that the High Court of Justice mentioned in the said Act shall be held in the Painted Chamber, in the Palace of Westminster on Wednesday the tenth day of this instant [i.e., present or current] January, by one o'clock in the afternoon. And this we do appoint to be notified by public proclaiming hereof in the great hall at Westminster, tomorrow being the ninth day of this instant January, betwixt the hours of nine and eleven in the forenoon. In testimony whereof we have hereunto set our hands and seals this eighth day of January, 1649.

We the commissioners whose names are hereunto subscribed, do hereby authorize and appoint Edward Dendy, sergeant at arms, to cause this to be proclaimed according to the tenor thereof, and to make due return of the same with this precept to the said Court at the time and place above-mentioned. [*List of names omitted.*] Which said precept is thus returned on the backside, *viz.* "I have caused due proclamation to be made hereof according to the tenor of the precept within written." *E. Dendy, Sergeant at Arms.*

And in order to the more regular and due proceedings of the said Court, they nominate officers and accordingly chose Mr. Aske, Dr. Dorislaus, Mr. Steel, and Mr. Cooke, counsel to attend the said Court [as well as] Mr. Greaves and Mr. John Phelps, clerks, to whom notice thereof was ordered to be given. Mr. Edward Walford, Mr. John Powel, Mr. John King, Mr. Phineas Payne, and Mr. Hull are chosen messengers to attend this Court.

Tuesday, January 9.
According to the precept of the eighth instant, Sergeant Dendy made proclamation for the sitting of the said Court in manner following, *viz.* About ten o'clock of the same day, the said sergeant being attended with six trumpets and a guard of two troops of horse, himself with them on horseback, bearing his mace, rides into the middle of Westminster Hall (the Court of Chancery then sitting […]) where, after the said trumpets sounding (the drums then likewise beating in the Palace Yard) he causes the said precept to be openly read, which being done, the House of Commons at the same time sitting, order as follows:

Ordered by the Commons assembled in parliament, that the same proclamation that was made this morning in Westminster Hall touching the trial of the king be made at the **Old Exchange** and in **Cheapside**, forthwith, and in the same manner, and that Sergeant Dendy, the sergeant at arms, do proclaim the same accordingly, and that the guard that lies in St. Paul's [churchyard] do see the same done.

In pursuance whereof Sergeant Dendy, about twelve o'clock of the same day, accompanied with ten trumpets and two troops of horse, drawn out for that purpose in St. Paul's churchyard, himself mounted, bearing his mace, they all march from thence unto the Old Exchange, London, where after the trumpets had sounded, he makes proclamation as he had done before in Westminster Hall. From thence they immediately march to Cheapside, making the like proclamation there also, in manner as aforesaid. During all which time the streets are thronged with spectators, without the least violence, injury, or affront publicly done or offered.

Wednesday, January 10.

The Court being sat in the place aforesaid began to take into consideration the manner and order that they intended to observe at the king's trial, and appointed two ushers of the Court, *viz.* Mr. Edward Walford and Mr. Vowell, and Mr. Litchman was chosen a messenger of this Court.

John Bradshaw, sergeant at law and a commissioner of this Court, was then chosen President of the said Court, who being absent, Mr. Say one of the commissioners then present, was appointed President *pro tempore* [temporarily] and until the said Sergeant Bradshaw should attend the said service, the said Mr. Say accordingly took his place, and gave the thanks of this Court to Mr. Garland, one of the commissioners of this Court, for his great pains formerly taken about the business of this Court.

The Court were informed of the great and important employment that at present lay upon Mr. Greaves in the behalf of the Commonwealth, from which he cannot be spared without prejudice to the public. It was therefore moved in his behalf that he might be excused from attending the service of one of the clerks of the said Court, which the Court admitted as a sufficient excuse, and thereupon Mr. Andrew Broughton was named and appointed one of the clerks of this Court with John Phelps, the said John Phelps being then sent for by a messenger of the Court, and accordingly making his appearance, was commanded to attend the said service, who attended the same accordingly, and a messenger of the Court was sent to summon the said Mr. Broughton.

Mr. Aske, Mr. Steel, Dr. Dorislaus, and Mr. Cooke are appointed counsel in the behalf of the Commonwealth, to prepare and prosecute the charge against the king according to the Act of the Commons assembled in parliament in that behalf, and in particular, the Court did appoint Mr. Steel, Attorney, and Mr. Cooke, Solicitor, to take care thereof. And the Act for constituting the said

Old Exchange, Cheapside:
Two busy commercial centres in the City of London, usual sites for public proclamations.

John Bradshaw (1602–59):
A one-time provincial lawyer and mayor; from 1643 a judge in London's sheriff's court, then appointed sergeant-at-law and Chief Justice of Chester.

Court was ordered to be transcribed and delivered to the said counsel, which was done accordingly.

Mr. Love, Mr. Lisle, Mr. Millington, Mr. Garland, Mr. Marten, Mr. Thomas Challoner, Sir John Danvers, and Sir Henry Mildmay, or any two of them, are appointed a committee to consider of all circumstances in matter of order and method for the carrying on and managing the king's trial, and for that purpose to advise with the counsel assigned, to prove the charge against the king and to make report therein the next sitting, and the care of the business is particularly recommended to Mr. Love.

Edward Dendy, sergeant at arms, made return of the precept of January 8, for proclaiming the sitting of the Court, which was received, the said Sergeant Dendy having proclaimed the same by the sound of trumpet in Westminster Hall, as also at the Old Exchange, and in Cheapside.

Edward Dendy, sergeant at arms, is appointed to attend the said Court. Mr. John King is appointed crier of the said Court.

The Court having thus made preparations for the said trial (during all which time they sat privately) the doors are now opened for all parties that had anything to do there to give their attendance. Three proclamations being made by the crier, the Act for constituting the said Court was openly read and the Court called. The commissioners present were as before named.

The commissioners that were absent were ordered to be summoned to attend the said service, and summonses were issued forth accordingly. The Court adjourned itself till Friday, January 12, at two o'clock in the afternoon, to the same place.

Friday, January 12
Sergeant Bradshaw, upon special summons, attended this Court, being one of the commissioners thereof, and being according to former order called to take his place of president of the said Court, made an earnest apology for himself to be excused. But therein not prevailing, in obedience to the commands and desires of this Court, he submitted to their order and took place accordingly. Thereupon the said Court ordered concerning him as follows, *viz.* that John Bradshaw, sergeant at law, who is appointed President of this Court, should be called by the name and have the title of Lord President, and that as well without as within the said Court, during the commission and sitting of the said Court. Against which title he pressed much to be heard to offer his exceptions, but was therein overruled by the Court.

Mr. Andrew Broughton attended according to former order, and it was thereupon again ordered that Andrew Broughton and John Phelps, gent., be and they are hereby constituted clerks of the said Court, and enjoined to give their attendance from time to time accordingly.

Ordered, that the counsel assigned, or such as they shall appoint, shall have power to search for all records and writings concerning the king's trial, and to take into their custody or order the producing of all such records and papers, or copies thereof, by any clerk or other person whatsoever, at or before the said trial, as they shall judge requisite, the said counsel giving a note under their hands of their receipt of all such original books and papers which they shall so take into their custody. And that the said counsel shall have power to send for such person or persons at or before the said trial, and to appoint by writing under their hands, their attendance for the service of the state in this business as they shall think requisite, requiring all persons concerned to yield obedience thereunto at their perils.

Sir Hardress Waller, knight, and Col. Harrison are ordered to desire the Lord General from time to time to appoint sufficient guards to attend and guard the said Court during their sitting.

Ordered, that Col. Tichbourne, Col. Roe, Mr. Blackiston, and Mr. Fry, members of this Court, shall make preparations for the trial of the king, that it may be performed in a solemn manner; and that they take care for other necessary provisions and accommodations in and about that trial, and are to appoint and command such workmen to their assistance as they shall think fit.

Mr. Love reports from the committee appointed Jan. 10 to consider of the circumstances in matters of order for trial of the king. And it is thereupon ordered, that in managing the proceedings in open court at the time of the king's trial, none of the Court do speak but the President and counsel, and in case of any difficulty arising to any one, that he speak not to the matter openly, but desire the President that the Court may please to advise. By which order, it is not intended that any of the commissioners be debarred at the examination of any witness to move the Lord President to propound such question to the witness as shall be thought meet for the better disquisition and finding out of the truth.

Ordered, that there shall be a Marshal to attend this Court, if there be cause.

Ordered, that the Lord President and counsel do manage the trial against the king according to instructions to be given them by the Court; and that the committee for considering of all circumstances for the managing of the king's trial do consider of rules and instructions in that behalf, and are to consult with the counsel and address themselves to the Lord President for advice in the premises.

Ordered, that the counsel do bring in the charge against the king on Monday next.

The committee for considering of the circumstances of order for the king's trial, together with Sir Hardress Waller, Col. Whaley, Mr. Scot, Col. Tichbourne, Col. Harrison, Lieut. Gen. Cromwell, and Col. Deane, are appointed to consider of the place for trying the king and to make report tomorrow in the afternoon, and are to meet tomorrow morning in the Inner Court of Wards, at nine o'clock, and who else of the Court please may be there. The Court adjourned itself till the morrow in the afternoon at two o'clock.

Saturday, January 13

Proclamation being made, and all parties concerned required to give attendance, the Court is called openly. The Court being [held] to make further preparations for the king's trial, sit privately. The sergeant at arms is authorized to employ such other messengers as shall be needful for the service of the Court, giving in their names to the clerks of this Court.

Ordered, that the sergeant at arms do **search and secure the vaults** under the Painted Chamber, taking such assistance therein from the soldiery as shall be needful.

Mr. Garland reports from the committee for considering of the place for the king's trial. The Court thereupon ordered that the said trial of the king shall be in Westminster Hall; that the place for the king's trial shall be where the Courts of King's Bench and Chancery sit in Westminster Hall, and that the partitions between the said two courts be therefore taken down; and that the committee for making preparations for the king's trial are to take care thereof accordingly.

The Court adjourned itself till Monday at two o'clock in the afternoon, to this place.

Monday, January 15.

Three proclamations are made and all parties concerned are required to give attendance.

The Court is called openly. The counsel attended and presented to the Court the draft of a charge against the king which, being read, the Court appointed Commissary General Ireton, Mr. Millington, Mr. Marten, Col. Harvey, Mr. Challoner, Col. Harrison, Mr. Miles Corbet, Mr. Scot, Mr. Love, Mr. Lisle, Mr. Say, or any three of them to be a committee, to whom the counsel might resort for their further advice concerning anything of difficulty in relation to the charge against the king; who were likewise with the counsel to compare the charge against him with the evidence, and to take care for the preparing and fitting the charge for the Court's more clear proceedings in the businesses; as likewise to advise of such general rules as are fit for expediting the business of the said Court, and to meet the morrow morning at eight o'clock in the Queen's Court.

Col. Ludlow, Col. Purefoy, Col. Hutchinson, Col. Scroope, Col. Deane, Col. Whalley, Col. Huson, Col. Pride, Sir Hardress Waller, and Sir William Constable, together with the committee for making preparations for the king's trial, or any three of them, are appointed a committee to consider of the manner of bringing the king to the Court at his trial, and of the place where he shall be kept and lodge at during his said trial; and to take consideration of the secure

search and secure the vaults: Presumably recollecting the Gunpowder Plot of 1605, in which Catholic conspirators placed barrels of gunpowder in the vaults under the parliament chamber with the intent to blow up the king and lords.

sitting of the said Court and placing the guards that shall attend it, and are to meet tomorrow morning at eight o'clock in the inner Star Chamber.

The Court taking notice of the nearness of **Hilary term** and necessity they apprehended of adjourning it in regard of the king's trial, thereupon were of opinion that it is fit that a fortnight of the said term be adjourned, and Mr. Lisle is desired to move the House therein.

Three proclamations. The Court adjourned itself till Wednesday next at eight in the morning.

Wednesday, January 17.
Three proclamations are made and all parties concerned are required to give attendance.

The Court is called.

Ordered, that the commissioners of this Court who have not hitherto appeared be summoned by warrants under the hands of the clerks of this Court to give their personal attendance at this Court, to perform the service to which they are by Act of the Commons of England assembled in parliament, appointed and required.

Ordered, that the sergeant at arms attending this Court, or his deputy, do forthwith summon all the aforesaid commissioners making default who reside or dwell within twenty miles of London.

Particular warrants to every one of them were accordingly issued forth for their attendance. Upon report made by Col. Hutchinson, from the committee to consider of the manner of bringing the king to trial, &c., the Court order as follows, *viz.*

Ordered, that **Sir Robert Cotton**'s house be the place where the king shall lodge during his trial; that the chamber in Sir Robert Cotton's house next to the study shall be the king's bed-chamber; that the great chamber before the said lodging chamber be for the king's dining room, and that a guard consisting of thirty officers and other choice men do always attend the king, who are to attend him at his lodging above stairs, and that two of the said thirty do always attend in his bed chamber; that place for a Court of Guard for 200 foot soldiers be built in Sir Robert Cotton's garden, near the waterside; that ten companies of foot be constantly upon the guards for securing Sir Robert Cotton's house, and those companies to be quartered in the Court of Requests, the Painted Chamber, and other necessary places thereabouts; that the passage that comes out of the Old Palace into Westminster Hall be made up at the entrance of the said passage next the said Guard; that the top of the stairs at the Court of Wards' door have a crossbar made to it; that the king be brought out of Sir Robert Cotton's house to his trial the lower way into Westminster Hall, and so brought to the bar in the face of the Court, attended by the above said guard above stairs; that two rails of about forty foot distance from the place where this Court shall sit in Westminster Hall be made across the said Hall, for the

Hilary term: The English legal year was (and still is) divided into four terms in which the courts sat, beginning in Michaelmas (October–December) and then proceeding through Hilary (January–April), Easter (April–May), and Trinity (June–July), with vacations in between.

Sir Robert Cotton: Cotton (1571–1631) had been a great book collector and antiquarian, gathering a formidable library in his house just north of Westminster Palace, which he opened to the use of fellow MPs, lawyers, and scholars until King Charles, who feared its seditious possibilities, forced him to close it. Cotton's grandson later bequeathed the collection to the nation, forming the basis of the British Library. The modern Houses of Parliament now cover the site of his house.

effectual and substantial doing whereof, this Court do refer it to the care of the committee appointed to consider of the manner of bringing the king to trial, who are likewise to take care for raising the floor in such part of the hall as they shall think fit for placing of the guards; and that a rail or rails from the Court down to the hall gate be made in such manner as they shall think fit on the Common Pleas side, to keep the people from the soldiers.

That there be guards set upon the leads [roofs] and other places that have windows to look into the Hall.

That the general be desired from time to time to send and appoint convenient guards of horse for the convenient sitting of the Court.

That twenty officers or other gentlemen do attend upon the Lord President from time to time, to and from this Court through Westminster Hall.

That the officers of the ordnance do send unto this Court 200 **halberds or partisans** lying within the Tower of London for the arming of the guards that are to attend this Court.

That at the time of the trial of the king, the commissioners do before their sitting in the Court meet in the Exchequer Chamber, and do from thence come up the Hall into the Court.

That all back doors from the house called **Hell** be stopped up during the king's trial.

That lodgings be prepared for the Lord President at Sir Abraham Williams's house in the New Palace Yard during the sitting of this Court, and that all provisions and necessaries be provided for his Lordship.

That Sir Henry Mildmay, Mr. Holland, and Mr. Edwards do take care for providing all provisions and necessaries for the king during his trial.

That Sir Henry Mildmay, Mr. Holland, and Mr. Edwards do likewise take care for all necessaries for the Lord President.

Ordered, that the committee for considering of the manner of bringing the king to trial do consider what habits [i.e., clothing or uniforms] the officers of this Court shall have, who are to advise with some heralds at arms therein, and concerning the ordering of the said officers.

That a sword be carried before the Lord President at the trial of the king.

That John Humphreys, esq., do bear the sword before the Lord President.

That a **mace** or maces together with a sword be likewise carried before the Lord President.

This Court doth adjourn itself to three o'clock in the afternoon, Jan. 17.

Three proclamations. The Court is cleared of strangers and they sit private.

The charge against the king is presented by the counsel and ordered to be re-committed to the committee appointed for advice with the counsel concerning the charge against the king, who are to contract the same, and fit it for the Court's proceeding thereupon, according to the Act of parliament in that behalf. And the same committee are likewise to take care for the king's coming to Westminster to trial at such time as to them shall seem meet, and Lieutenant Gen. Cromwell is added to the said committee, and the counsel are to attend this Court with the said charge tomorrow at two o'clock in the afternoon. And thereupon ordered that the committee for considering of the manner of bringing the king to trial do meet tomorrow morning at eight o'clock in the Exchequer Chamber.

The Court adjourned itself till the morrow at two o'clock in the afternoon, to the same place.

Thursday, January 18.
Three proclamations made. Here the Court sat private.

Col. Tichbourne, one of the commissioners of this Court, informs the Court that he was with Mr. Steel, attorney of this Court, and found him in his bed very sick, and by reason thereof not like to attend yet the service of this Court, according to former order; and desired him the said Colonel to signify that he the said Mr. Steel no way declines the service of the said Court out of any disaffection to it, but professes himself to be so clear in the business that if it should please God to restore him, he should manifest his good affection to the said cause, and that it is an addition to his affliction that he cannot attend this Court to do that service that they have expected from him and as he desires to perform.

The Court adjourned itself till tomorrow, two o'clock in the afternoon.

Friday, January 19.
Three proclamations. The Court called openly. Here the Court sat private.

Col. Hutchinson reports from the committee appointed to consider of the habits of the officers, and it is thereupon ordered that three gowns be provided for three ushers and three cloaks for three messengers of this Court.

Mr. Millington reports from the committee for advice with the counsel concerning the charge against the king that the counsel have perfected the charge and are ready to present it. He likewise reports the draft of an order whereby the charge may, by the command of this Court, be exhibited together with a form of words; the effect whereof the committee think fit to be pronounced by him that this Court shall appoint so to exhibit the said charge. Which said order and form of words the Court have with some alterations agreed unto, as follows;

It is ordered, that Mr. Attorney, and in his absence, Mr. Solicitor do in the behalf of the people of England exhibit and bring into this Court a charge of high treason and other high crimes against Charles Stuart, king of England, and charge him thereupon in the behalf aforesaid.

The form of words are as follows:

My Lord,
According to an order of this High Court to me directed for that purpose, I do, in the name and on the behalf of the people of England, exhibit and bring

into this Court a charge of high treason and other high crimes, whereof I do accuse Charles Stuart, king of England, here present. And I do, in the name and on the behalf aforesaid, desire the said charge may be received accordingly, and due proceedings had thereupon.

The counsel likewise, according to Mr. Millington's report, present a draft of the charge against the king, which was read the first and second and third time and referred back to the said counsel to make some small amendments as to the form thereof.

Ordered, that Commissary Gen. Ireton, Col. Whalley, Col. Harrison, Sir Hardress Waller, or any two of them, do appoint the thirty persons that are by order of Jan. 17 to attend the king and the twenty that are to attend the Lord President.

Ordered, that the sergeant at arms do secure Mr. Squibb's gallery by such ways and means as he shall conceive meet.

The Court adjourned itself until nine o'clock tomorrow morning.

Saturday, January 20.
Three proclamations, and attendance commanded.

Ordered, that Sir Henry Mildmay be desired to deliver unto John Humphreys, esq., the **sword of state** in his custody; which said sword the said Mr. Humphreys is to bear before the Lord President of this Court.

The Court being sat as aforesaid, before they engaged in further business, the sergeant at arms of the House of Commons came thither and acquainted the Court that the House wanted their members that were of that Court. The Court thereupon adjourned till twelve o'clock the same day. The Court accordingly met at twelve o'clock.

Three proclamations made. Here the Court sat private.

Ordered, that the form and method of the Court's proceeding unto and in the reading of the commission by which they sit, sending for and bringing in the prisoner to the bar, acquainting him in brief with the cause of his bringing thither, receiving and reading the charge, and demanding what the prisoner says thereto, be referred to the discretion of the Lord President; as also, that in case the prisoner shall in language or carriage towards the Court be insolent, outrageous, or contemptuous, that it be left to the Lord President to reprehend him therefore and admonish him of his duty, or to command the taking away of the prisoner, and if he see cause, to withdraw or adjourn the Court. But as to the prisoner's putting off his hat, the Court will not insist upon it for this day; and that if the king desire time to answer, the Lord President is to give him time.

Ordered, upon the Lord President's desire and motion, that Mr. Lisle and Mr. Say, commissioners of this Court, be assistants to the Lord President. For that purpose, it is ordered that they sit near the Lord President in Court.

sword of state: This symbolized the king's power against his enemies and to maintain law, and was carried before the king at great occasions of state such as the opening of parliaments.

Mr. Solicitor presented the charge against the king engrossed in parchment, which was read, and being by Mr. Solicitor signed, was returned to him to be exhibited against the king, in his presence in open court. And thereupon the Court adjourned itself forthwith to the great hall in Westminster.

The Manner of the Trial of Charles Stuart King of England.
On Saturday, being the 20 January 1649, the Lord President of the High Court of Justice, his two assistants, and the rest of the commissioners of the said Court, according to the adjournment of the said Court from the Painted Chamber, came to the bench, or place prepared for their sitting, at the west end of the great hall at Westminster. Divers officers of the said Court, 120 gentlemen with partisans, and a sword and mace marched before them up into the Court, where the Lord President, in a crimson velvet chair fixed in the midst of the Court, placed himself, having a desk with a crimson velvet cushion before him. The rest of the members placed themselves on each side of him, upon several seats or benches prepared, and hung with scarlet for that purpose. The Lord President's two assistants sitting next of each side of him, and the two clerks of the Court placed at a table somewhat lower, and covered with a Turkey carpet; upon which table was also laid the sword and mace, the said guard of partisans dividing themselves on each side of the Court before them.

Three proclamations are made for all persons that were adjourned over thither, to draw near. The Court being thus sat and silence enjoined, the great gate of the hall was set open, to the intent that all persons (without exception) desirous to see or hear might come unto it. Upon which the hall was presently filled, and silence again ordered and proclaimed.

After silence proclaimed as aforesaid, the Act of the Commons of England assembled in parliament, for erecting a High Court of Justice for trying and judging of Charles Stuart, king of England, was openly read by one of the clerks of the Court.

The Act being read, the Court was called, every commissioner present thereupon rising to his name. This done, the Court command the sergeant at arms to send for the prisoner. Thereupon, Col. Thomlinson, who had the charge of the prisoner, within a quarter of an hour's space brought him, attended by Col. Hacker and thirty two officers with partisans, guarding him to the Court, his own servants immediately attending him. Being thus brought up in the face of the Court, the sergeant at arms with his mace receives him, and conducts him straight to the bar, having a crimson velvet chair set before him. After a stern looking upon the Court and the people in the galleries on each side of him, he places himself in the chair, not at all moving his hat or otherwise showing the least respect to the Court; but presently rises up again, and turns about, looking downwards upon the guards placed on the left side and on the multitude of spectators on the right side of the said great hall. The guard that attended him in the meantime divided themselves on each side the court, and his own servants following him to the bar, stand on the left hand of the prisoner.

The prisoner having again placed himself in his chair, with his face towards the court, and silence being again ordered and proclaimed, the Lord President in the name of the court addressed himself to the prisoner, acquainting him that the Commons of England assembled in parliament, being deeply sensible of the evils and calamities that had been brought upon this nation, and of the innocent blood that had been spilt in it, which was fixed upon him as the principal author of it, had resolved to make inquisition for this blood, and according to the debt they did owe to God, to justice, the kingdom, and themselves, and according to that fundamental power that rested, and trust reposed in them by the people, other means failing through his default, had resolved to bring him to trial and judgment, and had therefore constituted that Court of Justice, before which he was then brought, where he was to hear his charge, upon which the Court would proceed according to justice.

Hereupon, Mr. Cooke, solicitor for the Commonwealth, standing within a bar, with the rest of the counsel for the Commonwealth on the right hand of the prisoner, offered to speak. But the prisoner, having a staff in his hand, held it up and softly laid it upon the said Mr. Cooke's shoulder two or three times, bidding him hold. Nevertheless, the Lord President ordering him to go on, Mr. Cooke did according to the order of the Court to him directed, in the name and on the behalf of the people of England, exhibit a charge of high treason and other high crimes, and did therewith accuse the said Charles Stuart, king of England; praying in the name, and on the behalf aforesaid, that the charge might be accordingly received and read, and due proceedings had thereupon; and accordingly preferred a charge in writing, which being received by the Court and delivered to the clerk of the Court, the Lord President in the name of the Court ordered it should be read.

But the king interrupting the reading of it, the Court notwithstanding commanded the clerk to read it, acquainting the prisoner that if he had anything to say after, the Court would hear him. Whereupon the clerk read the charge, the tenor whereof is as follows, *viz.*

A Charge of High Treason, and other High Crimes Exhibited to the High Court of Justice by John Cooke, Esq., Solicitor General, appointed by the said Court, for, and on the behalf of the People of England, against Charles Stuart, king of England:

That he the said Charles Stuart, being admitted king of England, and therein trusted with a limited power to govern by and according to the laws of the land and not otherwise; and by his trust, oath and office, being obliged to use the power committed to him for the good and benefit of the people, and for the preservation of their rights and liberties; yet, nevertheless, out of a wicked design to erect and uphold in himself an unlimited and tyrannical power to rule according to his will, and to overthrow the rights and liberties of the people, yea to take away and make void the foundations thereof, and of all redress and remedy of misgovernment, which by the fundamental constitutions of this kingdom were reserved on the people's behalf, in the right and power of frequent and successive parliaments or national meetings in council, he the said Charles Stuart, for accomplishment of such his designs, and for the protecting of himself and his adherents, in his and their wicked practices, to the same ends, has traitorously and maliciously levied war against the present parliament and the people therein represented.

Particularly, upon or about June 30, in the year of our Lord 1642, at Beverley in the county of York; and upon or about July 30 in the year aforesaid, in the county of the city of York; and upon or about August 24 in the same year, at the county of the town of Nottingham, where, and when he set up his standard of war. And also on or about October 23 in the same year, at Edge Hill and Kineton Field, in the county of Warwick; and upon or about the November 30 in the same year, at Brainford in the county of Middlesex; and upon or about August 30, in the year of our Lord 1643, at Caversham Bridge near Reading in the county of Berks; and upon or about October 30 in the year last mentioned, at or near the city of Gloucester; and upon or about November 30 in the year last mentioned, at Newbury in the county of Berks; and upon or about July 31 in the year of our Lord 1644, at Cropredy Bridge in the county of Oxon; and upon or about September 30 in the last year mentioned, at Bodmin and other places near adjacent, in the county of Cornwall; and upon or about November 30 in the year last mentioned, at Newbury aforesaid; and upon or about June 8 in the year of our Lord 1645 at the town of Leicester; and also upon the 14th day of the same month in the same year, at Naseby Field in the county of Northampton. At which several times and places, or most of them, and at many other places in this land, at several other times within the years aforementioned, and in the year of our Lord 1646, he the said Charles Stuart has caused and procured many thousands of the free people of this nation to be slain, and by divisions, parties, and insurrections within this land, by invasions from foreign parts, endeavoured and procured by him, and by many other evil ways and means, he the said Charles Stuart has not only maintained and carried on the said war both by land and sea, during the year before mentioned, but also has renewed or caused to be renewed the said war against the parliament and good people of this nation, in this present year 1648, in the counties of Kent, Essex, Surrey, Sussex, Middlesex, and many other counties and places in England and Wales, and also by sea. And particularly he the said Charles Stuart has for that purpose given commission to his son the prince, and others, whereby, besides multitudes of other persons, many such as were by the parliament intrusted and employed for the safety of the nation (being by him or his **angels** corrupted to the betraying of their trust, and revolting from the parliament) have had entertainment and commission for the continuing and renewing of war and hostility against the said parliament and people, as aforesaid.

angels: Phelps's original has "agents" here.

By which cruel and unnatural wars by him the said Charles Stuart levied, continued, and renewed as aforesaid, much innocent blood of the free people of this nation has been spilt, many families have been undone, the public treasury wasted and exhausted, trade obstructed and miserably decayed, vast expense and damage to the nation incurred, and many parts of this land spoiled, some of them even to desolation. And for further prosecution of his said evil designs, he the said Charles Stuart does still continue his commissions to the said prince and other rebels and revolters, both English and foreigners, and to the Earl of Ormond and to the Irish rebels and revolters associated with him, from whom further invasions upon this land are threatened, upon the procurement and on the behalf of the said Charles Stuart.

All which wicked designs, wars, and evil practices of him the said Charles Stuart have been and are carried on for the advancement and upholding of a personal interest of will and power, and pretended prerogative to himself and his family, against the public interest, common right, liberty, justice, and peace of the people of this nation, by and for whom he was intrusted as aforesaid.

By all which it appears that he the said Charles Stuart has been and is the occasioner, author, and continuer of the said unnatural, cruel, and bloody wars, and therein guilty of all the treasons, murders, **rapines**, burnings, spoils, desolations, damages, and mischiefs to this nation acted and committed in the said wars, or occasioned thereby.

And the said John Cooke by protestation saving on the behalf of the said people of England the liberty of exhibiting at any time hereafter any other charge against the said Charles Stuart, and also of replying to the answers which the said Charles Stuart shall make to the premises, or any of them, or any other charge that shall be so exhibited, does for the said treasons and crimes, on the behalf of the said people of England, impeach the said Charles Stuart as a tyrant, traitor, murderer, and a public and implacable enemy to the Commonwealth of England, and pray that the said Charles Stuart, king of England, may be put to answer all and every [of] the premises, and that such proceedings, examinations, trials, sentences and judgments may be thereupon had, as shall be agreeable to justice. Subscribed, John Cooke.

The prisoner, while the charge was reading, sat down in his chair, looking sometimes on the High Court and sometimes on the galleries, and rose again and turned about to behold the guards and spectators, and after sat down looking very sternly, and with a countenance not at all moved, till these words, *viz. CHARLES STUART to be a tyrant, traitor,* &c. were read; at which he laughed as he sat in the face of the Court.

The charge being read, the Lord President, in the name of the Court, demanded the prisoner's answer thereto. But the prisoner declining that, fell into a discourse of the late treaty in the Isle of Wight, and demanded, by what lawful authority he was brought from the Isle thither, upbraiding the Court with the many unlawful authorities in the world, instancing robbers and takers of purses, pleading his kingship, and thereby a trust committed to him by God, by descent, which he should betray, together with the liberties of the people, in case he should answer to an unlawful power, which he charged the Court to be, and that they were raised by an usurped power; and affirmed, that he stood more for the liberties of the people than any of the judges there sitting, and again demanded, by what authority he was brought thither?

To which it was replied by the Court that had he been pleased to have observed what was declared to him by the Court at his first coming, and the charge which he had heard read unto him, he might have informed himself by what authority he was brought before them, namely, by the authority of the Commons of England assembled in parliament, on the behalf of the people of England; and did therefore again several times advise him to consider of a better answer, which he refused to do, but persisted in his **contumacy**. Whereupon the Court at length told him that they did expect from him a positive answer to the charge, affirming their authority, and giving him to understand that they were upon God's and the kingdom's errand, and that the peace stood for would be better had and kept when justice was done, and that was their present work. [The Court] advised him seriously to consider what he had to do at his next appearance, which was declared should be upon Monday following, and so remanded him to his former custody.

The prisoner, all the time having kept on his hat, departed without showing any the least respect to the Court. But going out of the bar, said, he did not fear that bill, pointing to the table where the sword and charge lay.

The prisoner being withdrawn, three proclamations were made, and the Court adjourned itself to the Painted Chamber on Monday morning then next, at nine o'clock, declaring that from thence they intended to adjourn to the same place again.

**[What follows between these asterisks and the next is an insertion made by Nalson, drawing from Mabbott, but with some edits of his own, shown in italics. One exception: whereas Mabbott used Bradshaw's title, Lord President, in Nalson's borrowing, it is simply "Bradshaw."]

But that the reader may have the entire relation of this deplorable tragedy, I have from the most authentic prints inserted at large the interlocutory passages between the king and Bradshaw, of which Mr. Phelps in his journal gives only a succinct account; which take as follows:

His Majesty with his wonted patience, heard all these slanders and reproaches, sitting in the chair and looking sometimes on the pretended Court, sometimes up to the galleries, and rising again, turned about to behold the guards and spectators. Then he sat down with a majestic and unmoved countenance, and sometimes smiling, especially at those words [tyrant, traitor,] and the like. Also the silver head of his

contumacy: Obstinate refusal to obey a court order.

*staff happened to fall off, at which he wondered; and seeing none to take it up, he
stooped for it himself.*

The charge being read, Bradshaw began.

Sir, You have now heard your charge read, containing such matters as appear
in it: You find that in the close of it, it is prayed to the Court, in the behalf of
the Commons of England, that you answer to your charge. The Court expects
your answer.

King: I would know by what power I am called hither. I was not long ago in
the Isle of Wight, how I came there is a longer story than I think is fit at this
time for me to speak of, but there I entered into a treaty with both Houses of
Parliament, with as much public faith as it's possible to be had of any people
in the world. I treated [negotiated] there with a number of honourable lords
and gentlemen, and treated honestly and uprightly. I cannot say but they did
very nobly with me. We were upon a conclusion of the treaty. Now I would
know by what authority (I mean lawful; there are many unlawful authorities in
the world—thieves and robbers by the high-ways—but I would know by what
authority) I was brought from thence, and carried from place to place, and I
know not what. And when I know by what lawful authority, I shall answer.

Remember, I am your king, your lawful king, and what sins you bring upon
your heads and the judgment of God upon this land. Think well upon it, I say,
think well upon it, before you go further from one sin to a greater. Therefore let
me know by what lawful authority I am seated here, and I shall not be unwilling
to answer. In the meantime, I shall not betray my trust; I have a trust committed
to me by God, by old and lawful descent. I will not betray it to answer to a new
unlawful authority. Therefore, resolve me that, and you shall hear more of me.

Bradshaw: If you had been pleased to have observed what was hinted to you by
the Court at your first coming hither, you would have known by what authority;
which authority requires you in the name of the people of England, of which
you are elected king, to answer.

King: No, Sir, I deny that.

Bradshaw: If you acknowledge not the authority of the Court, they must proceed.

King: I do tell them so: England was never an elective kingdom, but an hereditary
kingdom for near these thousand years. Therefore let me know by what authority
I am called hither. I do stand more for the liberty of my people than any here
that come to be my pretended judges. And therefore let me know by what lawful
authority I am seated here, and I will answer it; otherwise I will not answer it.

Bradshaw: Sir, how really you have managed your trust, is known. Your way of answer is to interrogate the Court, which beseems not you in this condition. You have been told of it twice or thrice.

King: Here is a gentleman, Lieut. Col. Cobbet, ask him if he did not bring me from the Isle of Wight by force. I do not come here as submitting to the Court. I will stand as much for the privilege of the House of Commons, rightly understood, as any man here whatsoever: I see no House of Lords here, that may constitute a parliament; and the king too should have been [here]. Is this the bringing of the king to his parliament? Is this the bringing an end to the treaty in the public faith of the world? Let me see a legal authority warranted by the Word of God, the Scriptures, or warranted by the constitutions of the kingdom, and I will answer.

Bradshaw: Sir, you have propounded a question, and have been answered. Seeing you will not answer, the Court will consider how to proceed. In the meantime, those that brought you hither are to take charge of you back again. The Court desires to know whether this be all the answer you will give, or no.

King: Sir, I desire that you would give me and all the world satisfaction in this. Let me tell you, it is not a slight thing you are about. I am sworn to keep the peace, by that duty I owe to God and my country; and I will do it to the last breath of my body. And therefore you shall do well to satisfy first God and then the country by what authority you do it. If you do it by a usurped authority, you cannot answer it. There is a God in Heaven that will call you, and all that give you power, to account. Satisfy me in that, and I will answer; otherwise I betray my trust, and the liberties of the people. And therefore think of that, and then I shall be willing. For I do avow that it is as great a sin to withstand lawful authority, as it is to submit to a tyrannical, or any other ways unlawful authority. And therefore satisfy God, and me, and all the world in that, and you shall receive my answer. I am not afraid of the bill.

Bradshaw: The Court expects you should give them a final answer. Their purpose is to adjourn till Monday next. If you do not satisfy yourself, though we do tell you our authority, we are satisfied with our authority; and it is upon God's authority and the kingdom's. And that peace you speak of, will be kept in the doing of justice, and that's our present work.

King: For answer, let me tell you, you have shown no lawful authority to satisfy any reasonable man.

Bradshaw: That's in your apprehension; we are satisfied that are your judges.

King: 'Tis not my apprehension, nor yours neither, that ought to decide it.

Bradshaw: The Court has heard you, and you are to be disposed of as they have commanded.

So commanding the guard to take him away, His Majesty only replied, Well, Sir. And at his going down, pointing with his staff toward the axe, he said, I do not fear that. As he went down the stairs, the people in the hall cried out, God save the King, notwithstanding some were set there by the faction to lead the clamour for justice.[1] **

Painted Chamber, January 22.
Here the Court sat private.

Ordered, that the committee for nominating the officers of this Court, together with the committee for nominating the guards, do consider of an allowance for diet of the officers, and what other satisfaction they shall have for their service.

Col. Harvey informs the Court that he was desired to signify, in the behalf of Mr. John Corbet, member of this Court, that his absence is not from any disaffection to the proceedings of this Court, but in regard of other especial employment that he has in the service of the state.

Here the Court considered of the king's carriage on the Saturday before, and of all that had then passed on the Court's behalf, and approved thereof, as agreeing to their sense and directions. And perceiving what the king aimed at, *viz* to bring in question (if he could) the jurisdiction of the Court and the authority whereby they sat; and considering that he had not in the interim acknowledged them in any sort to be a Court, or in any judicial capacity to determine of his demand and plea, and that through their sides he intended to wound (if he might be permitted) the supreme authority of the commons of England, in their representative. The Commons assembled in parliament, after advice with their counsel learned in both laws and mature deliberation had of the matter, resolved that the prisoner should not be suffered to bring these things in question which he aimed at, touching that highest jurisdiction, whereof they might not make themselves judges, and from which there was no appeal. And therefore order and direct, *viz*.

Ordered, that in case the king shall again offer to fall into that discourse, the Lord President do let him know that the Court have taken into consideration his demands of the last day, and that he ought to rest satisfied with this answer, that the Commons of England assembled in parliament have constituted this

---

1   This is a paraphrase of what Mabbott wrote here: "It is to be observed that as the charge was reading against the king, the head of his staff fell off, which he wondered at. And seeing none to take it up, he stoops for it himself. As the king went away, facing the court, he said 'I do not fear that' (meaning the sword). The people in the hall, as he went down the stairs, cried out, some, 'God save the King' and most for 'Justice.'"

Court, whose power may not nor should not be permitted to be disputed by him, and that they were resolved he should answer his charge.

That, in case he shall refuse to answer or acknowledge the Court, the Lord President do let him know that the Court will take it as a contumacy, and that it shall be so recorded.

That, in case he shall offer to answer with a saving notwithstanding of his pretended prerogative, that the Lord President do in the name of the Court refuse his protest and require his positive answer to the charge.

That, in case the king shall demand a copy of the charge, that he shall then declare his intention to answer; and that declaring such his intention, a copy be granted unto him.

That, in case the king shall still persist in his contempt, the Lord President do give command to the clerk to demand of the king in the name of the Court, in these words following, *viz.* Charles Stuart, king of England, you are accused in the behalf of the people of England of diverse high crimes and treasons, which charge has been read unto you. The Court requires you to give a positive answer, whether you confess or deny the charge, having determined that you ought to answer the same.

Ordered, that the commissioners shall be called in open Court, at the Court's sitting in the Hall, and that the names of such as appear shall be recorded.

Hereupon, the Court forthwith adjourned itself into Westminster Hall.

Westminster Hall, 22 January Afternoon.
The commissioners coming from the Painted Chamber take their place in the public court in Westminster Hall, as on Saturday before. And being sat, and the Hall doors set open, three proclamations are made for all persons that were adjourned over to this time to give their attendance, and for all persons to keep silence upon pain of imprisonment.

The Court is thereupon called. The Court being called, the sergeant is commanded to fetch his prisoner. The king is again brought prisoner to the bar, as on Saturday before. Proclamation is made for silence whilst pleas of the Commonwealth were in hand, and order given to the captain of the guard to take into his custody such as should disturb the Court.

Mr. Solicitor moved the Court that the prisoner might give a positive answer to his charge, or otherwise that the Court would take the matter of it *pro confesso* [as if confessed] and proceed thereupon according to justice; which being pressed by the Court upon the prisoner, and their judgment again made known unto him, that he was to answer his charge, otherwise that his contumacy would be recorded.

The prisoner, that notwithstanding, still insisted upon his former plea and that the Court had no power, nor the commons of England who had constituted it, to proceed against him. Upon which, the clerk of the Court, by command and according to former order, required his answer in the form prescribed. And the prisoner still refusing to submit thereto, his default and contempt were again recorded, the prisoner remanded, and the Court adjourned itself till the next day, being Tuesday, at twelve o'clock, to the Painted Chamber; withal, giving notice, that from thence they intended to adjourn to this place again.

**[Nalson's interpolation, between these asterisks and the next, is drawn from Mabbott, with his own additions in italics.]

Sunday having been spent in fasting and seditious preaching, according to the mode of these impious hypocrites, who used to preface rebellion and murder with the appearance of religion. The illustrious sufferer was (as is before in Phelps's journal related) placed before the infamous tribunal; where their mercenary Solicitor Cooke opened the tragic scene thus, displaying his talents of impudence and treason.

Cooke: May it please your Lordship, my Lord President, I did at the last Court, in the behalf of the commons of England, exhibit and give in to this Court a charge of high treason and other high crimes against the prisoner at the bar; whereof I do accuse him in the name of the people of England. And the charge was read unto him, and his answer required. My Lord, he was not pleased to give an answer; but instead of answering, did there dispute the authority of this High Court. My humble motion to this High Court, in the behalf of the kingdom of England, is, that the prisoner may be directed to make a positive answer, either by way of confession or negation; which, if he shall refuse to do, that then the matter of charge may be taken *pro confesso*, and the Court may proceed according to justice.

Bradshaw: Sir, you may remember, at the last court you were told the occasion of your being brought hither, and you heard a charge read against you, containing a charge of high treason and other high crimes against this realm of England. You have heard likewise that it was prayed in the behalf of the people that you should give an answer to that charge, that thereupon such proceedings might be had as should be agreeable to justice. You were then pleased to make some scruples concerning the authority of this Court, and knew not by what authority you were brought hither. You did divers times propound your questions, and were as often answered, that it was by authority of the Commons of England assembled in parliament, that did think fit to call you to account for those high and capital misdemeanors wherewith you were then charged.

Since that, the Court has taken into consideration what you then said: they are fully satisfied with their own authority, and they hold it fit you should stand satisfied with it too. And they do require it, that you do give a positive and particular answer to this charge that is exhibited against you. They do expect you should either confess or deny it: If you deny, it is offered in the behalf of the kingdom, to be made good against you. Their authority they do avow to the whole world, that the whole kingdom are to rest satisfied in, and you are to rest satisfied with it. And therefore you are to lose no more time, but to give a positive answer thereunto.

King: When I was here last, 'tis very true, I made that question. And if it were only my own particular case, I would have satisfied myself with the protestation I made the last time I was here, against the legality of this Court, and that a king cannot be tried by any superior jurisdiction on Earth: But it is not my case alone, it is the freedom and the liberty of the people of England. And do you pretend what you will, I stand more for their liberties. For if power without law may make laws, may alter the fundamental laws of the kingdom, I do not know what subject he is in England that can be sure of his life or anything that he calls his own. Therefore, when that I came here, I did expect particular reasons, to know by what law, what authority you did proceed against me here; and therefore I am a little to seek what to say to you in this particular, because the affirmative is to be proved, the negative often is very hard to do. But since I cannot persuade you to do it, I shall tell you my reasons as short as I can.

My reasons why in conscience and the duty I owe to God first and my people next, for the preservation of their lives, liberties and estates, I conceive I cannot answer this, till—

Bradshaw: Sir, I must interrupt you; which I would not do, but that what you do is not agreeable to the proceedings of any court of justice. You are about to enter into argument and dispute concerning the authority of this Court, before whom you appear as a prisoner and are charged as an high delinquent. If you take upon you to dispute the authority of the Court, we may not do it, nor will any court give way unto it. You are to submit unto it, you are to give a punctual and direct answer, whether you will answer your charge or no, and what your answer is.

King: Sir, by your favour, I do not know the forms of law; I do know law and reason, though I am no lawyer professed: but I know as much law as any gentleman in England, and therefore, under favour, I do plead for the liberties of the people of England more than you do. And therefore if I should impose a belief upon any man without reasons given for it, it were unreasonable. But I must tell you, that by that reason that I have, as thus informed, I cannot yield unto it.

Bradshaw: Sir, I must interrupt you; you may not be permitted. You speak of law and reason; it is fit there should be law and reason; and there is both against you. Sir, the vote of the Commons of England assembled in parliament it is the reason of the kingdom; and they are these too that have given that law according to which you should have ruled and reigned. Sir, you are not to dispute our authority, you are told it again by the Court. Sir, it will be taken notice of that you stand in contempt of the Court, and your contempt will be recorded accordingly.

King: I do not know how a king can be a delinquent; but by any law that ever I heard of, all men (delinquents, or what you will) let me tell you, they may put in **demurrers** against any proceeding as legal. And I do demand that, and demand to be heard with my reasons: if you deny that, you deny reason.

demurrer: A legal pleading that even if the alleged facts are true, there is no legal basis for a case at law.

Bradshaw: Sir, you have offered something to the Court; I shall speak something unto you the sense of the Court. Sir, neither you nor any man are permitted to dispute that point; you are concluded, you may not demur to the jurisdiction of the Court. If you do, I must let you know that they overrule your demurrer. They sit here by the authority of the commons of England, and all your predecessors and you are responsible to them.

King: I deny that; show me one precedent.

Bradshaw: Sir, you ought not to interrupt while the Court is speaking to you. This point is not to be debated by you, neither will the Court permit you to do it. If you offer it by way of demurrer to the jurisdiction of the Court, they have considered of their jurisdiction, they do affirm their own jurisdiction.

King: I say, Sir, by your favour, that the Commons of England was never a court of judicature. I would know how they came to be so.

Bradshaw: Sir, you are not to be permitted to go on in that speech and these discourses.

Then the clerk of the Court read, Charles Stuart, king of England, you have been accused on the behalf of the people of England of high treason and other high crimes; the Court have determined that you ought to answer the same.

King: I will answer the same so soon as I know by what authority you do this.

Bradshaw: If this be all that you will say, then, gentlemen, you that brought the prisoner hither, take charge of him back again.

King: I do require that I may give in my reasons why I do not answer; and give me time for that.

Bradshaw: Sir, 'tis not for prisoners to require.

King: Prisoners, Sir! I am not an ordinary prisoner.

Bradshaw: The Court has considered of their jurisdiction, and they have already affirmed their jurisdiction. If you will not answer, we will give order to record your default.

King: You never heard my reasons yet.

Bradshaw: Sir, your reasons are not to be heard against the highest jurisdiction.

King: Show me that jurisdiction where reason is not to be heard.

Bradshaw: Sir, we show it you here, the Commons of England: and the next time you are brought, you will know more of the pleasure of the Court and, it may be, their final determination.

King: Show me where ever the House of Commons was a court of judicature of that kind.

Bradshaw: Sergeant, take away the prisoner.

King: Well, Sir, remember that the king is not suffered to give in his reasons for the liberty and freedom of all his subjects.

Bradshaw: Sir, you are not to have liberty to use this language. How great a friend you have been to the laws and liberties of the people, let all England and the world judge.

King: Sir, under favour, it was the liberty, freedom, and laws of the subject that ever I took——defended myself with arms: I never took up arms against the people, but for the laws.

Bradshaw: The command of the Court must be obeyed: no answer will be given to the charge.

King: Well, Sir.**

Then Bradshaw ordered the default to be recorded and the contempt of the court, and that no answer would be given to the charge. The king was guarded forth to Sir Robert Cotton's house. The Court adjourned to the Painted Chamber on

Tuesday at twelve o'clock, and from thence they intend to adjourn to Westminster Hall, at which time all persons concerned are to give their attendance.

Painted Chamber, Tuesday, January 23.
Three proclamations are made, and all parties concerned required to give their attendance.

Here the Court sat private. And taking into consideration the proceeding of the last Court the last day, fully approved of what in their behalf had been then said and done; and likewise taking into consideration the demeanour of the king at the said Court, have notwithstanding resolved to try him once more, whether he will own the Court; and to that purpose,

Ordered, that the Lord President do acquaint the king, in case he shall continue contumacious, that he is to expect no further time; and that the Lord President do therefore in the name of the Court require his positive and final answer. And if he shall still persist in his obstinacy, that the Lord President give command to the clerk to read as follows, *viz.*

Charles Stuart, king of England, you are accused on the behalf of the people of England, of divers high crimes and treasons, which charge has been read unto you. The Court now requires you to give your final and positive answer by way of confession or denial of the charge.

Nevertheless, if the king should submit to answer, and desire a copy of his charge, that it be granted him by the Lord President; notwithstanding, giving him to know that the Court might in justice forthwith proceed to judgment for his former contumacy and failure to answer, and that he be required to give his answer to the said charge the next day at one o'clock in the afternoon.

Whereupon the Court adjourned to Westminster Hall forthwith.

Westminster Hall, 23 January Afternoon.
Three proclamations being made, and attendance and silence commanded as formerly, the Court is thereupon called. The Court being called, the sergeant is required to send for the prisoner, who was accordingly brought to the bar, where he took his seat as formerly. Proclamation is thereupon made for silence while the pleas of the Commonwealth are in hand, and the captain of the guard commanded by proclamation to take into custody all that shall disturb the proceedings of the Court.

Mr. Solicitor Cooke, addressing himself to the Court, repeated the former delays and contempts of the prisoner, so as that no more needed on his part but to demand judgment; yet offered notwithstanding the notoriety of the facts charged, mentioned in the Commons' Act appointing the trial, to prove the truth of the same by witnesses, if thereto required; and therefore prayed, and yet (he said) not so much he, as the innocent blood that had been shed, the cry whereof was very great, that a speedy sentence and judgment might be pronounced against the prisoner at the bar according to justice.

Hereupon the Court putting the prisoner in mind of former proceedings, and that although by the rules of justice, if advantage were taken of his past contempts, nothing would remain but to pronounce judgment against him, they had nevertheless determined to give him leave to answer his charge; which, as was told him in plain terms (for justice knew no respect of persons) to plead *Guilty* or *Not Guilty* thereto.

To which he made answer as formerly, that he would not acknowledge the jurisdiction of the Court, and that it was against the fundamental laws of the kingdom; that there was no law to make a king a prisoner; that he had done nothing against his trust; and issued out into such like discourses.

Upon which, the Court's resolution was again remembered to him, and he told, that he had now the third time publicly disowned and affronted the Court; that how good a preserver he had been of the fundamental laws and freedoms of the people, his actions had spoken; that men's intentions were used to be showed by their actions, and that he had written his meaning in bloody characters throughout the kingdom, and that he should find at last, though at present he would not understand it, that he was before a court of justice.

Hereupon, in the manner appointed, the clerk in the name of the Court demanding the prisoner's answer to his charge, and the same refused, the default was recorded, the prisoner remanded, and the Court adjourned to the Painted Chamber.

Painted Chamber.
The Court according to their former adjournment from Westminster Hall, came together from thence into the Painted Chamber where they sat privately and ordered as follows,

Ordered, that no commissioner ought or shall depart from the Court without the special leave of the said Court.

This Court took into consideration the managing of the business of the Court this day, in the Hall, and the king's refusal to answer, notwithstanding he had been three several times demanded and required thereunto, and have thereupon fully approved of what on the Court's part had then passed, and resolved, that, notwithstanding the said contumacy of the king and refusal to plead, which in law amounts to standing mute and a tacit confession of the charge, and notwithstanding the notoriety of the fact charged, the Court would nevertheless however examine witnesses, for the further and clearer satisfaction of their own judgments and consciences; the manner of whose examination was referred to further consideration the next sitting, and warrants were accordingly issued forth for summoning of witnesses.

Mr. Peters moves the Court as a messenger from the king, viz. That the king desires he might speak with his chaplains that came unto him privately; but the House of Commons having taken that into their consideration, the Court conceived it not proper for them to intermeddle therein.

The Court adjourned itself till nine o'clock tomorrow morning, to this place.

**[Nalson's interpolation, between these asterisks and the next, is again drawn primarily from Mabbott, but with Nalson's own additions in italics.]

What passed in the Hall more at large than is related by Phelps in this day's transactions, see in the following discourse:

The king being brought in by the guard looks with a majestic countenance upon his pretended judges and sits down.

After the second O Yes, and silence commanded, Cooke began more insolently:

Cooke: May it please your Lordship, My Lord President, this is now the third time, that, by the great grace and favour of this High Court, the prisoner has been brought to the bar, before any issue joined in the cause. My Lord, I did at the first Court exhibit a charge against him, containing the highest treason that ever was wrought upon the theatre of England, that a king of England, trusted to keep the law, that had taken an oath so to do, that had tribute paid him for that end, should be guilty of a wicked design to subvert and destroy our laws and introduce an arbitrary and tyrannical government in the defiance of the parliament and their authority, set up his standard for war against the parliament and people. And I did humbly pray, in the behalf of the people of England, that he might speedily be required to make an answer to the charge. But, my Lord, instead of making any answer, he did then dispute the authority of this High Court. Your Lordship was pleased to give him a further day to consider and to put in his answer; which day being yesterday, I did humbly move that he might be required to give a direct and positive answer, either by denying or confession of it. But, my Lord, he was then pleased for to demur to the jurisdiction of the Court, which the Court did then overrule, and command him to give a direct and positive answer.

My Lord, besides this great delay of justice, I shall now humbly move your Lordship for speedy judgment against him. My Lord, I might press your Lordship upon the whole, that according to the known rules of the law of the land, that, if a prisoner shall stand as contumacious in contempt and shall not put in an issuable plea, guilty or not guilty of the charge given against him, whereby he may come to a fair trial, that as by an implicit confession it may be taken *pro confesso*, as it has been done to those who have deserved more favour than the prisoner at the bar has done. But besides, my Lord, I shall humbly press your Lordship upon the whole fact. The House of Commons, the supreme authority and jurisdiction of the kingdom, they have declared that it is notorious that the matter of the charge is true; as it is in truth, My Lord, as clear as crystal, and as the sun that shines at noon day: which, if your Lordship and the Court be not satisfied in, I have notwithstanding, on the people of England's behalf, several witnesses to produce. And therefore I do humbly pray (and yet I must confess, it is not so much I, as the innocent blood that has been shed, the cry whereof is very great for justice and judgment; and therefore I do humbly pray) that speedy judgment be pronounced against the prisoner at the bar.[2]

Bradshaw went on in the same strain: Sir, you have heard what is moved by the counsel on the behalf of the kingdom against you. Sir, you may well remember, and if you do not, the Court cannot forget what dilatory dealings the Court has found at your hands. You were pleased to propound some questions; you have had your resolution upon them. You were told over and over again that the Court did affirm their own jurisdiction; that it was not for you nor any other man to dispute the jurisdiction of the supreme and highest authority of England, from which there is no appeal, and touching which there must be no dispute. Yet you did persist in such carriage as you gave no manner of obedience, nor did you acknowledge any authority in them, nor the High Court that constituted this court of justice.

Sir, I must let you know from the Court, that they are very sensible of these delays of yours and that they ought not, being thus authorized by the supreme court of England, to be thus trifled withal; and that they might in justice, if they pleased, and according to the rules of justice, take advantage of these delays and proceed to pronounce judgment against you. Yet nevertheless they are pleased to give direction, and on their behalves I do require you, that you make a positive answer unto this charge that is against you. Sir, in plain terms (for justice knows no respect of persons) you are to give your positive and final answer in plain English, whether you be guilty or not guilty of these treasons laid to your charge.

The king, after a little pause, said, When I was here yesterday, I did desire to speak for the liberties of the people of England; I was interrupted. I desire to know yet whether I may speak freely or not.

Bradshaw: Sir, you have had the resolution of the Court upon the like question the last day. And you were told that having such a charge of so high a nature against you, your work was that you ought to acknowledge the jurisdiction of the Court and to answer to your charge. Sir, if you answer to your charge,

---

2   Solicitor Cooke had prepared a substantial case for the prosecution that he was not able to use in court, as Charles refused to enter the plea needed for a trial to begin. Cooke did publish it, however, as *King Charls his Case* (London, 1649).

which the Court gives you leave now to do, though they might have taken the advantage of your contempt; yet, if you be able to answer to your charge, when you have once answered, you shall be heard at large, make the best defence you can. But, Sir, I must let you know from the Court, as their commands, that you are not to be permitted to issue out into any other discourses till such time as you have given a positive answer concerning the matter that is charged upon you.

not a rush: A traditional expression meaning that something is of little value or significance.

King: For the charge, I value it **not a rush**. It is the liberty of the people of England that I stand for. For me to acknowledge a new court that I never heard of before, I that am your king, that should be an example to all the people of England, for to uphold justice, to maintain the old laws, indeed I know not how to do it. You spoke very well the first day that I came here on Saturday, of the obligations that I had laid upon me by God to the maintenance of the liberties of my people; the same obligation you spoke of, I do acknowledge to God, that I owe to Him and to my people, to defend as much as in me lies the ancient laws of the kingdom. Therefore until that I may know that this is not against the fundamental laws of the kingdom, by your favour, I can put in no particular answer. If you will give me time, I will show you my reasons why I cannot do it; and this—

Here being interrupted, he said, By your favour, you ought not to interrupt me. How I came here I know not. There's no law for it, to make your king your prisoner. I was in a treaty upon the public faith of the kingdom; that was the known——two Houses of Parliament, that was the representative of the Kingdom; and when that I had almost made an end of the treaty, then I was hurried away and brought hither; and therefore—

Bradshaw: Sir, you must know the pleasure of the Court.

King: By your favour, Sir.

Bradshaw: Nay, Sir, by your favour, you may not be permitted to fall into those discourses. You appear as a delinquent. You have not acknowledged the authority of the Court. The Court craves it not of you; but once more they command you to give your positive answer. Clerk, do your duty.

King: Duty, Sir!

The clerk reads: Charles Stuart, king of England, you are accused, in the behalf of the Commons of England, of divers high crimes and treasons; which charge has been read unto you. The Court now requires you to give your positive and final answer by way of confession or denial of the charge.

King: Sir, I say again to you, so that I might give satisfaction to the people of England, of the clearness of my proceeding, not by way of answer, not in this way, but to satisfy them, that I have done nothing against that trust that has been committed to me, I would do it; but to acknowledge a new court against their privileges, to alter the fundamental laws of the kingdom, Sir, you must excuse me.

Bradshaw: Sir, this is the third time that you have publicly disowned this Court and put an affront upon it. How far you have preserved the privileges of the people, your actions have spoken it. But truly, Sir, men's intentions ought to be known by their actions: You have written your meaning in bloody characters throughout the whole kingdom. But, Sir, you understand the pleasure of the Court.

Clerk: Record the default. And, gentlemen, you that took charge of the prisoner, take him back again.

King: I will only say this one word more to you: if it were only my own particular, I would not say any more, nor interrupt you.

Bradshaw: Sir, you have heard the pleasure of the Court and you are (notwithstanding you will not understand it) to find that you are before a court of justice.

Then the King went forth with the guard. And proclamation was made, that all persons which had then appeared and had further to do at the Court might depart into the Painted Chamber, to which place the Court did forthwith adjourn, and intended to meet at Westminster Hall by ten o'clock next morning.

Cryer: God bless the kingdom of England!**

Wednesday, January 24
Painted Chamber. Three proclamations made. The Court took into consideration the manner how the witnesses should be examined; and in regard the king has not pleaded to issue, and that this examination was ***ex abundanti***, only for the further satisfaction of themselves, resolved that the witnesses shall be examined to the charge against the king in the Painted Chamber, before the Court there. Ordered, That Mr. Millington and Mr. Thomas Challoner do forthwith repair unto John Brown, esq., clerk of the House of Peers for such papers as are in his custody, which are conducible for the business and service of this Court, and the said Mr. Brown is required to send the said papers hither accordingly.

ex abundanti: Out of abundance or more than necessary; often seen as "ex abundanti cautela," meaning from an abundance or excess of caution.

Witnesses produced and sworn in Court to give evidence to the charge against the king. [*29 names listed*]. Col. Horton, Col. Deane, Col. Okey, Col. Huson, Col. Roe, Col. Tichbourne, Col. Whalley, Col. Tomlinson, Col. Goffe, Col. Ewers, Col. Scroope, Mr. Love, Mr. Scot, Mr. Thomas Challoner, Mr. Millington, and Sir John Danvers, or any three of them, are a committee appointed to take the examination of the said witnesses now sworn, whom the clerks are to attend for that purpose. The Court granted their summons for summoning further witnesses and adjourned itself till the morrow at nine o'clock in the morning to this place.

Thursday, 25 January 1649.
Here the Court sat private. The Court ordered that the Marshal General of this army or his deputy do bring forthwith Mr. Holder, prisoner at Whitehall, to the end that he may testify his knowledge of all such matters as shall be propounded unto him concerning the charge against the king.

Ordered, that the dean's house in Westminster Abbey be provided and furnished for the lodging of the Lord President and his servants, guards, and attendants; and a committee are appointed to take care hereof accordingly.

Mr. Henry Gouge and Mr. William Cuthbert, witnesses produced to the charge against the king, were sworn and examined. The witnesses sworn in open court, and after[wards] examined by the committee appointed for that purpose the 24th instant, were now in open court called and their respective depositions were read to them, who did avow their said several depositions and affirm what was so read unto them respectively was true, upon the oaths they had taken.

The Court being informed that Major Fox, being of the guard attending the Lord President, is arrested and committed to the keeper of Ludgate [gaol], ordered that the said keeper do forthwith bring the said major before this Court, and attend this Court in person himself.

Mr. Holder being brought before this Court according to the order of this day, and his oath tendered unto him, to give evidence to such matters as should be propounded unto him concerning the charge against the king, the said Mr. Holder desired to be spared from giving evidence against the king. Whereupon, the Commissioners finding him already a prisoner, and perceiving that the questions intended to be asked him tended to accuse himself, thought fit to waive his examination, and remanded him (and accordingly did so) to the prison from whence he was brought.

The depositions taken *ut supra* [as above], are as follows, *viz.* 25 January 1649:

William Cuthbert of Patrington in Holderness, gentleman, aged 42 years or thereabouts, sworn and examined, says that he, living at Hull Bridge near Beverley, in July 1642, did then hear that forces were raised, about 3000 foot for the king's guard under Sir Robert Strickland. And this deponent further says that about 2 July 1642, he saw a troop of horse come to Beverley, being the Lord's Day, about four or five o'clock in the afternoon, called the Prince's Troop, Mr. James Nelthorp being then major of the said town. And this deponent further says that he did see that afternoon the said troop march from Beverley into Holderness, where they received ammunition brought up by the River of Humber unto them.

And this deponent further says that the same night, being Sunday, there came about 300 foot soldiers (said to be Sir Robert Strickland's regiment) under the command of Lieutenant Col. Duncombe and called the King's Guard, unto this deponent's house, called Hull Bridge, near Beverley, about midnight, and broke open, entered, and possessed themselves of the said house. And that the Earl of Newport, the Earl of Carnarvon, and divers others came that night thither to the said forces. And that the same night (as this deponent was then informed) Sir Thomas Gower, then High Sheriff of the said county, came thither, and left there a warrant for staying all provisions from going to Hull to Sir John Hotham; which warrant was then delivered to this deponent, being constable, by Lieut. Col. Duncombe.

And this deponent further says that he was by the said forces put out of his house, and did with his family go to Beverley; and that after that, (*viz.*) the Thursday following, to this deponent's best remembrance, he did see the king come to Beverley, to the Lady Gee's house there, where he, this deponent, did often see the king, with **Prince Charles** and the **Duke of York**. And the trained bands were then raised in Holderness, who were raised (as was generally reported) by the king's command.

And this deponent further says that the night after the said forces had possessed themselves of this deponent's house, Col. Legard's house was plundered by them, being upon a Monday; which entry of this deponent's house was the first act of hostility that was committed in those parts. This deponent further says that after the said Sir Robert Strickland's said company was gone from Hull Bridge, having continued there about ten days, there then came to the said house Col. Wivel, with about 700 foot soldiers, who then took up his quarters at Hull Bridge. And this deponent further says that the warrant he now produces to this Court is the same original warrant aforesaid spoken of. And this deponent further says that the general's name of the said forces that were there, and raised as aforesaid, was the Earl of Lindsey; and that this deponent was brought before the said general, in the name of the King's Lord General, for holding intelligence with Sir John Hotham, then governor of Hull; and because it was then informed to the general, that he this deponent had provisions of corn to send over unto Ireland, which this deponent was forbidden by the said general to send unto Ireland or any place else, without his or the king's direction or warrant first had in that behalf.

Prince Charles, Duke of York: The two oldest sons of the king, Charles and James.

The aforesaid warrant mentioned in the deposition of William Cuthbert is as follows: It is His Majesty's command that you do not suffer any victuals or provision of what sort soever to be carried into the town of Hull without His Majesty's special license first obtained; and of this you are not to fail at your peril. Dated at Beverley, 3 July 1642. Thomas Gower, to all head constables and constables in the East Riding of the County of York, and to all other His Majesty's loyal subjects.

John Bennet of Harewood, in the county of York, glover, sworn and examined, says that he being a soldier under the king's command, the first day that the king's standard was set up at Nottingham, which was about the middle of summer last was six years, he did work at Nottingham, and that he did see the king within the Castle of Nottingham, within two or three days after the standard was so set up, and that the standard did fly the same day that the king was in the castle, as aforesaid, and this deponent did hear that the king was at Nottingham the same day that the standard was first set up, and before.

And this deponent further says that he, and the regiment of which he then was, had their colours then given them. And Sir William Pennyman, being the colonel of the said regiment, was present with his regiment at that time. And this deponent further says that there was then there the Earl of Lindsey's regiment, who had then their colours given them, and that the said Earl of Lindsey was then also proclaimed there the king's general; and that it was proclaimed then there likewise in the king's name, at the head of every regiment, that the said forces should fight against all that came to oppose the king or any of his followers; and in particular, against the **Earl of Essex**, the Lord Brooke, and divers others; and that the said Earl of Essex and Lord Brooke and divers others were then proclaimed traitors, and that the same proclamations were printed and dispersed by the officers of the regiments throughout every regiment.

And this deponent further says that the standard was advanced upon the highest tower of Nottingham Castle; and that he did see the king often in Nottingham at that time that the forces continued at Nottingham, they continuing there for the space of one month; and that the drums for raising volunteers to fight under the king's command were then beaten all the said county over, and divers other forces were raised there. And this deponent further says that he did take up arms under the king's command for fear of being plundered, Sir William Pennyman giving out that it were a good deed to fire the said town because they would not go forth in the king's service, and that this deponent's father did thereupon command him to take up arms, and that divers others (as they did confess) did then also take up arms for the king for fear of being plundered.

And this deponent further says that in or about the month of October 1642 he did see the king at Edge Hill in Warwickshire, where he sitting on horseback while his army was drawn up before him, did speak to the colonel of every regiment that passed by him, that he would have them speak to their soldiers

Earl of Essex: Robert Devereux, Earl of Essex was the first chief commander of the parliamentarian army, before Thomas Fairfax and Oliver Cromwell came to prominence with parliament's New Model Army.

to encourage them to stand it, and to fight against the Earl of Essex, the Lord Brookes, Sir William Waller, and Sir William Balfour. And this deponent says that he did see many slain at the fight at Edge Hill, and that afterwards he did see a list brought in unto Oxford of the men which were slain in that fight; by which it was reported, that there were slain 6559 men. And this deponent further says afterwards, in or about the month of November 1642, he did see the king in the head of his army at Hounslow Heath in Middlesex, **Prince Rupert** then standing by him. And he, this deponent, did then hear the king encourage several regiments of Welshmen (then being in the field) which had run away at Edge Hill, saying unto them that he did hope they would regain their honour at Brentford, which they had lost at Edge Hill.

William Brayne of Whixhall in the County of Salop [Shropshire], gentleman, being sworn and examined, deposes that about August 1642, this deponent saw the king at Nottingham, while the standard was set up and the flag flying. And that he much about the same time marched with the king's army from Nottingham to Derby, the king himself being then in the army. And about September the said year, this deponent was put upon his trial at Shrewsbury as a spy, before Sir Robert Heath and other commissioners of **oyer and terminer**, the king then being in person in Shrewsbury.

Henry Hartford of Stratford upon Avon in Warwickshire, sworn and examined, deposes that about corn harvest in 1642, this deponent saw the king in Nottingham Castle, while the standard was set upon one of the towers of the Castle, and the flag flying. And he further says and deposes that he saw the king the same year about the month of November in Brainford Town on horseback, with a great many commanders about him, on a Sunday morning, when on the Saturday night before, there were a great many of the parliament's forces slain by the king's forces in the said town.

Robert Lacy of the town and county of Nottingham, painter, sworn and examined, deposes that he in summer time in 1642, by order from my Lord Beaumont, did paint the standard pole which was set up on the top of the old tower of Nottingham Castle. And he further says that he saw the king in the town of Nottingham diverse times while the standard was up there and the flag flying, and the king did lie at the house of my Lord of Clare in Nottingham Town, and that he this deponent did then and there see the king many times.

Edward Roberts of Bishop Castle in the County of Salop, ironmonger, sworn and examined, says and deposes that he saw the king in Nottingham Town while the standard was set upon the high tower in Nottingham Castle. And he further says that he saw the king at the head of the army at Shrewsbury, upon the march towards Edge Hill, and that he likewise saw the king in the rear of his army in Kineton Field; and likewise saw the king upon the Sunday morning at Brainford, after the fight upon the Saturday next before, in the said town.

Prince Rupert: The son of Charles's sister Elizabeth and her husband, the Elector Palatine, Prince Rupert of the Rhine had gained martial experience in the Thirty Years' War on the Continent and came to help his uncle in his wars, becoming commander of the royalist cavalry at age 23.

oyer and terminer: Commissions authorizing judges to "hear and determine" criminal cases.

Robert Loads of Cottam in Nottinghamshire, tile maker, sworn and examined, says that he, about October 1642, saw the king in the rear of his army in Kineton Field upon a Sunday, where he saw many slain on both sides. And he further says that he saw the king in Cornwall in his army, near the house of my Lord Mohun, about Lostwithiel, about corn harvest 1644.

Samuel Morgan of Wellington in Shropshire, felt maker, sworn and examined, deposes that he upon a Sunday morning in Kineton Field saw the king upon the top of Edge Hill in the head of the army, some two hours before the fight, which happened after Michaelmas on a Sunday, 1642. And he saw many men killed on both sides in the same time and place. And he further says that in the year 1644, he saw the king in his army near Cropredy Bridge, where he saw the king light off his horse and draw up the body of his army in person himself.

James Williams of Ross in Herefordshire, shoemaker, sworn and examined, deposes that about October 1642, he saw the king in Kineton Field below the hill in the field with his sword drawn in his hand, at which time and place there was a great fight, and many killed on both sides. And he further deposes that he saw the king at Brainford on a Sunday in the forenoon, in November, while the king's army was in the town and round about it.

John Pyneger of the parish of Heanor in the county of Derby, yeoman, aged 37 years or thereabout, sworn and examined, says that about August 1642, he saw the king's standard flying upon one of the towers of Nottingham Castle. Upon the same day he saw the king in Thurland House, being the Earl of Clare's house in Nottingham, in the company of Prince Rupert, Sir John Digby, and other persons, both noblemen and others. And that the King had at the same time in the said town a train of artillery, and the town was then full of the king's soldiers.

Samuel Lawson of Nottingham, maltster, aged 30 years or thereabouts, sworn and examined, says that about August 1642, he saw the king's standard brought forth of Nottingham Castle, borne upon diverse gentlemen's shoulders (who as the report was) were noblemen, and he saw the same by them carried to the hill close adjoining to the castle, with a herald before it, and there the standard was erected with great shoutings, acclamations, and sound of drums and trumpets, and that when the standard was so erected, there was a proclamation made, and that he saw the king present at the erecting thereof. And this deponent further says that the town was then full of the king's soldiers, of which some quartered in this deponent's house, and that when the king with his forces went from the town, the inhabitants of the town were forced to pay a great sum of money to the king's army, being threatened that in case they should refuse to pay it, the town should be plundered.

Arthur Young, citizen and barber surgeon of London, being aged 29 years or thereabouts, sworn and examined, says that he was present at the fight at Edge Hill between the king's army and the parliament's, in October 1642, and he did then see the king's standard advanced and flying in his army in the fight. And that he did then take the king's standard in that battle from the king's forces, which was afterwards taken from him by one Middleton, who was afterwards made a colonel.

Thomas Whittington of the town and county of Nottingham, shoemaker, aged 22 years, sworn and examined, says that he saw the king in the town of Nottingham, the same day that his standard was first set up in Nottingham Castle, being about the beginning of August 1642, and that the king then went from his lodgings at Thurland House towards the castle; and that he, this deponent, saw him several times about that time in Nottingham, there being divers soldiers at that time in the town who were called by the name of the king's soldiers. And this deponent further says that he saw the king's standard flying upon the old tower in the castle.

John Thomas of Llangollen in the county of Denbigh, husbandman, aged 25 years or thereabouts, sworn and examined, says that he saw the king at Brainford in the county of Middlesex, on a Saturday night at twelve o'clock, soon after Edge Hill fight, attended with horse and foot soldiers, the king being then on horseback with his sword by his side. And this deponent then heard the king say to the soldiers as he was riding through the said town, "Gentlemen, you lost your honour at Edge Hill, I hope you will regain it again here," or words to that effect. And this deponent further says that there were some skirmishes between the king's army and the parliament's army at the same time, both before and after the king spoke the said words, and that many men were slain on both sides.

Richard Blomfield, citizen and weaver of London, aged 35 years or thereabouts, sworn and examined, says that at the defeat of the Earl of Essex's army in Cornwall, he this deponent was there, it being at the latter end of the month of August, or beginning of September 1644. At which time, he saw the king at the head of his army, near Foy, on horseback, and further says that he did then see divers of the Lord of Essex's soldiers plundered, contrary to **articles** then lately made, near the person of the king.

articles: The articles, or terms, upon which one party agreed to surrender to the other.

William Jones of Uske in the county of Monmouth, husbandman, aged 22 years or thereabouts, sworn and examined, says that he did see the king within two miles of Naseby Field, the king then coming fromwards Harborough, marching in the head of his army, towards Naseby Field where the fight was; and that he did then see the king ride up to the regiment which was Col. St. George's, and there the deponent did hear the king ask the regiment, Whether they were willing to fight for him? To which the soldiers made an acclamation, crying, All, All. And this deponent further says that he saw the king in Leicester with his forces, the same day that the king's forces had taken it from the parliament's forces. And this deponent further says that he saw the king in his army that besieged Gloucester at the time of the siege.

Humphrey Browne of Whissendine in the county of Rutland, husbandman, aged 22 years or thereabouts, sworn and examined, says that at such time as the town of Leicester was taken by the king's forces, being in or about June 1645, Newark Fort in Leicester was surrendered to the king's forces upon composition, that neither clothes nor money should be taken away from any of the soldiers of that fort which had so surrendered, nor any violence offered to them; and that as soon as the said fort was upon such composition so surrendered, the king's soldiers contrary to the articles fell upon the soldiers of the said fort, stripped, cut, and wounded many of them; whereupon, one of the king's officers rebuking some of those that did so abuse the parliament's soldiers, this deponent did then hear the king reply, "I do not care if they cut them three times more, for they are mine enemies," or words to that effect. The king was then on horseback, in bright armour, in the said town of Leicester.

David Evans of Abergavenny in the county of Monmouth, smith, aged about 23 years, sworn and examined, says that about half an hour before the fight at Naseby, about midsummer in June 1645, he saw the king marching up to the battle in the head of his army, being about half a mile from the place where the said battle was fought.

Diogenes Edwards of Carston in the county of Shropshire, butcher, aged 21 years or thereabouts, sworn and examined, says that in June 1645, he did see the king in the head of his army, an hour and a half before the fight in Naseby Field, marching up to the battle, being then a mile and a half from the said field. And this deponent says that he did afterwards the same day see many slain at the said battle.

Giles Gryce of Wellington in Shropshire, gentleman, sworn and examined, deposes that he saw the king in the head of his army at Cropredy Bridge, with his sword drawn in his hand, that day when the fight was against Sir William Waller, on a Friday, as this deponent remembers, in the year 1644, about the month of July, and he further says that he saw the king in the same summer, in Cornwall, in the head of his army, about Lostwithiel at such time as the Earl of Essex was there with his army. And he further says that he also saw the king in the head of his army, at the second fight near Newbury. And further says that he saw the king in the front of the army in Naseby Field, having back and breast on [i.e., partial armour]. He further says that he saw the king in the head of the army, at what time the town of Leicester was stormed, and saw the king ride into the town of Leicester, after the town was taken, and he saw a great many men killed on both sides, at Leicester, and many houses plundered.

John Vinson of Damerham in Wiltshire, gentleman, sworn and examined, says that he did see the king at the first Newbury fight, about the month of September 1643 in the head of his army, where this deponent did see many slain on both sides. This deponent also says that he did see the king at the second battle at Newbury, about the month of November 1644 where the king was at the head of his army in complete armour with his sword drawn. This deponent did then see the king lead up Colonel Thomas Howard's regiment of horse, and did hear him make a speech to the soldiers, in the head of that regiment, to this effect, that is to say, that the regiment should stand to him that day, for that his crown lay upon the point of the sword, and if he lost that day, he lost his honour and his crown for ever. And that this deponent did see many slain on both sides at this battle. This deponent further says that he did see the king in the battle at Naseby Field, in Northamptonshire, on or about the month of June 1645, where the king was then completely armed with back, breast and helmet, and had his sword drawn, where the king himself after his party was routed, did rally up the horse and caused them to stand. At that time this deponent did see many slain on both sides.

George Seely of London, cordwainer [shoemaker], sworn and examined, says that he did see the king at the head of a brigade of horse at the siege of Gloucester, and did also see the king at the first fight at Newbury, about the month of September 1643 where the king was at the head of a regiment of horse. There were many slain at that fight on both sides. This deponent also says that he did see the king at the second fight at Newbury, which was about November 1644, where the king was in the middle of his army.

John Moore of the city of Cork in Ireland, gentleman, sworn and examined, says that at the last fight at Newbury, about the month of November 1644, he did see the king in the middle of the horse, with his sword drawn, and that he did see abundance of men at that fight slain upon the ground, on both sides. This deponent also says that he did see the king ride into Leicester, before a party of horse, the same day that Leicester was taken by the king's forces, which was about the month of June 1645. This deponent further says that he did see the king before the fight at Leicester, at Cropredy Bridge, in the midst of a regiment of horse, and that he did see many slain at the same time, when the king was in the fight at Cropredy Bridge. And lastly, this deponent says that he did see the king at the head of a regiment of horse at Naseby fight about the month of June 1645, where he did see abundance of men cut, shot, and slain.

Thomas Ives of Boyset, in the county of Northampton, husbandman, sworn and examined, says that he did see the king in his army at the first fight of Newbury, in Berkshire, in the month of September 1643, and that he did see many slain at that fight, he and others with a party of horse being commanded to face the parliament's forces, whilst the foot did fetch off the dead. He says also that he did see the king advance with his army to the fight at Naseby Field in Northamptonshire, about June 1645, and that he did again at that fight see the king come off with a party of horse after that his army was routed in the field, and that there were many men slain on both parts, at that battle at Naseby.

Thomas Rawlins of Hanslope in the county of Buckingham, gentleman, sworn and examined, says that he did see the king near Fowey in Cornwall in or about the month of July 1644 at the head of a party of horse. And this deponent did see some soldiers plunder after the articles of agreement made between the king's army and the parliament's forces, which soldiers were so plundered by the king's party, not far distant from the person of the king.

Thomas Read of Maidstone in the county of Kent, gentleman, sworn and examined, says that presently after the laying down of arms in Cornwall, between Lostwithiel and Fowey, in or about the latter end of the month of August or the beginning of September 1644, he did see the king in the head of a guard of horse.

James Crosby of Dublin in Ireland, barber, sworn and examined, says that at the first fight at Newbury, about the time of barley harvest 1643, he did see the king riding from Newbury town, accompanied with divers lords and gentlemen, towards the place where his forces were then fighting with the parliament's army.

Samuel Burden of Lyneham in the county of Wilts, gentleman, sworn and examined, says that he was at Nottingham in or about the month of August 1642, at which time he saw a flag flying upon the tower of Nottingham Castle. The next day afterwards he did see the king at Nottingham, when the flag was still flying, which flag this deponent then heard was the king's standard. He says also that he did afterwards see the king at Cropredy Bridge in the head of his army, in a fallow field there, and did see the king in pursuit of Sir William Waller's army, being then routed, which was about the month of July 1644. And at that time this deponent did see many people slain upon the ground. And further this deponent says that in or about the month of November 1644, he did see the king at the last fight at Newbury, riding up and down the field from regiment to regiment, whilst his army was there fighting with the parliament's forces. And this deponent did see many men slain at that battle on both sides.

Michael Potts of Sharperton in the county of Northumberland, vintner [wine merchant], sworn and examined, deposes that he saw the king in the head of the army in the fields about a mile and a half from Newbury town, upon the heath, the day before the fight was, it being about harvest tide in the year 1643. And he further says that he saw the king on the day after, when the fight was, standing near a great piece of ordnance in the fields. And he further says that he saw the king in the second Newbury fight in the head of his army, being after or about Michaelmas 1644. And he further says that he saw a great many men slain at both the said battles. And he further says that he saw the king in the head of his army near Cropredy Bridge in the year 1644. And he further says that he saw the king in the head of his army in Cornwall, near Lostwithiel, while the Earl of Essex lay there with his forces, about the middle of harvest 1644.

George Cornwall of Aston in the county of Hereford, ferryman, aged 50 years or thereabouts, sworn and examined, says that he did see the king near Cropredy Bridge, about the time of mowing of corn, 1644, in the van of the army there, and that he drew up his army upon a hill and faced the parliament's army; and that there was thereupon a skirmish between the king's and the parliament's army, where he, this deponent, saw divers persons slain on both sides.

The examination of Henry Gooche of Grays Inn in the county of Middlesex, gentleman, sworn and examined: this deponent says that upon or about 30 September last, he was in the Isle of Wight and had access unto and discourse with the king, by the means of the Lord Marquess of Hartford and Commissary Morgan, where this deponent told the king that his majesty had many friends; and that since his majesty was pleased to justify the parliament's first taking up arms, the most of the Presbyterian party, both soldiers and others, would stick close to him. To which the king answered thus, that he would have all his old friends know, that though for the present he was contented to give the parliament leave to call their own war what they pleased, yet that he neither did at that time nor ever should decline the justice of his own cause. And this deponent told the king that his business was much retarded, and that neither Col. Thomas nor any other could proceed to action through want of commission. The king answered that he being upon a treaty would not dishonour himself; but that if he, this deponent, would take the pains to go over to the prince his son (who had full authority from him), he the said deponent, or any for him, should receive whatsoever commissions should be desired. And to that purpose, he would appoint the Marquess of Hartford to write to his son in his name, and was pleased to express much of joy and affection, that his good subjects would engage themselves for his restoration.

Robert Williams of the parish of St. Martins in the county of Cornwall, husbandman, aged 23 years or thereabouts, sworn and examined, says that he did see the king marching in the head of his army about September 1644, a mile from Lostwithiel in Cornwall in armour, with a short coat over it unbuttoned. And this deponent further says that he saw him after that in St. Austell Downs, drawing up his army. And this deponent says he did after that see the king in the head of his army near Fowey, and that the Earl of Essex and his army did then lie within one mile and a half of the king's army.

The witnesses being examined as aforesaid, the Court adjourned for an hour.

January 25, 1649. Afternoon.
Richard Price of London, scrivener, was produced a witness to the charge against the king, who being sworn and examined, says that upon occasion of some tampering by the king's agents with the **Independents** in and about London, to draw them from the parliament's cause to the king's party; and this being discovered by some of those so tampered with unto sundry members of the **Committee of Safety**, who directed a carrying on of a seeming compliance with the king, this deponent did travel to Oxford, in January 1643, having a safe conduct under the king's hand and seal, which this deponent knows to be so, for that the king did own it when he was told that this deponent was the man that came to Oxfordshire with that safe conduct.

Independents: A loose grouping rather than a political party, the Independents were one of two broad factions that emerged in the years of fighting, set against the Presbyterians in advocating more complete religious toleration and the separation of Church and State, whereas the Presbyterians wanted to replace one national church with another.

Committee of Safety: A committee of MPs charged with overseeing the parliamentary war effort.

And this deponent also says that after sundry meetings between him and the Earl of Bristol about the drawing of the Independents unto the king's cause against the parliament, the substance of the discourse, at which meetings the Earl told this deponent, was communicated to the king, this deponent was by the Earl brought to the king to confer further about that business; where the king declared that he was very sensible that the Independents had been the most active men in the kingdom for the parliament against him; and thereupon persuaded this deponent to use all means to expedite their turning to him and his cause. And for their better encouragement, the king promised in the word of a king that if they, the Independents, would turn to him and be active for him against the parliament, as they had been active for them against him, then he would grant them whatsoever freedom they would desire. And the king did then refer this deponent unto the Earl of Bristol for the further prosecuting of the said business.

And the Earl thereupon (this deponent being withdrawn from the king) did declare unto this deponent, and willed him to impart the same unto the Independents for their better encouragement, that the king's affairs prospered well in Ireland; that the Irish subjects had given the rebels (meaning the parliament's forces) a great defeat; that the king had sent the Lord Byron with a small party towards Cheshire, and that he was greatly multiplied and had a considerable army and was then before Nantwich, and would be strengthened with more soldiers out of Ireland, which were come and expected daily. And when this deponent was to depart out of Oxford, four safe conducts with blanks in them, for the inserting of what names this deponent pleased, were delivered to him under the king's hand and seal. And one Ogle was sent out of Oxford with this deponent, to treat about the delivering up of Aylesbury to the king, it being then a garrison for the parliament, and at the same time Oxford was a garrison for the king.

Several papers and letters of the king's, under his own hand and of his own writing, and other papers are produced and read in open court. Mr. Thomas Challoner also reports several papers and letters of the king's writing and under the king's own hand.

After which the Court sat private. The Court taking into consideration the whole matter in charge against the king passed these votes following, as preparatory to the sentence against the king, but ordered that they should not be binding finally to conclude the Court, *viz.*,

Resolved upon the whole matter, that this Court will proceed to sentence of condemnation against Charles Stuart, king of England. Resolved, &c. that the condemnation of the king shall be for a tyrant, traitor and murderer. That the condemnation of the king shall be likewise for being a public enemy to the Commonwealth of England. That this condemnation shall extend to death.

Memorandum, the last aforementioned commissioners were present at these votes.

The Court being then moved concerning the deposition and deprivation of the king before, and in order to that part of his sentence which concerned his execution, thought fit to defer the consideration thereof to some other time, and ordered the draft of a sentence grounded upon the said votes to be accordingly prepared by Mr. Scot, Mr. Marten, Col. Harrison, Mr. Lisle, Mr. Say, Commissary Gen. Ireton and Mr. Love, or any three of them, with a blank for the manner of his death.

Ordered, that the members of this Court who are in and about London and are not now present be summoned to attend the service of this Court tomorrow at one o'clock in the afternoon; for whom summons were issued forth accordingly.

The Court adjourned itself till the morrow at one o'clock in the afternoon.

Friday, 26 January 1649, Afternoon.
Painted Chamber. Three proclamations. The Court called. Here the Court sat private.

The draft of a sentence against the king is according to the votes of 25 January prepared and, after several readings, debates, and amendments by the Court thereupon, resolved, &c. that this Court do agree to the sentence now read; that the said sentence shall be **engrossed**; [and] that the king be brought to Westminster tomorrow, to receive his sentence.

engrossed: Written out formally.

The Court adjourned itself till the morrow at ten o'clock in the morning to this place; the Court giving notice that they then intended to adjourn from thence to Westminster Hall.

Saturday, 27 January 1649.
Painted Chamber. Three proclamations being made, the Court is thereupon called.
The sentence agreed on and ordered by this Court, to be engrossed, being accordingly engrossed, was read.

Resolved, that the sentence now read shall be the sentence of this Court for the condemnation of the king, which shall be read and published in Westminster Hall this day.

The Court hereupon considered of certain instructions for the Lord President, to manage the business of this day in Westminster Hall, and ordered,

That the Lord President do manage what discourse shall happen between him and the king, according to his discretion, with the advice of his two assistants; and that in case the king shall still persist in excepting against the Court's jurisdiction, to let him know that the Court do still affirm their jurisdiction.

That, in case the king shall submit to the jurisdiction of the Court, and pray a copy of the charge, that then the Court do withdraw and advise.

That, in case the king shall move anything else worth the Court's consideration, that the Lord President upon advice of his said assistants do give order for the Court's withdrawing to advise.

That, in case the king shall not submit to answer, and there happen no such cause of withdrawing, that then the Lord President do command the sentence to be read; but that the Lord President should hear the king say what he would before the sentence, and not after.

And thereupon it being further moved, whether the Lord President should use any discourse or speeches to the king, as in the case of other prisoners to be condemned was usual before the publishing of the sentence, received general directions to do therein as he should see cause, and to press what he should conceive most seasonable and suitable to the occasion. And it was further directed that after the reading of the sentence, the Lord President should declare that the same was the sentence, judgment, and resolution of the whole Court, and that the commissioners should thereupon signify their consent by standing up. The Court forthwith adjourned itself to Westminster Hall.

January 27, 1649. Afternoon. Westminster Hall.
The Lord President and the rest of the commissioners come together from the Painted Chamber to Westminster Hall, according to their adjournment, and take their seats there, as formerly. Three proclamations being made for attendance and silence, the Court is called.

The prisoner is brought to the bar, and proclamation is again (as formerly) made for silence, and the captain of the guard ordered to take into his custody all such as should disturb the Court.

The President stood up, with an intention of address to the people and not to the prisoner, who had so often declined the jurisdiction of the Court; which the prisoner observing, moved he might be heard before judgment given; whereof he received assurance from the Court that he should be heard after he had heard them first.

Whereupon the Court proceeded, and remembered [reminded] the great assembly then present of what had formerly passed betwixt the Court and the prisoner, the charge against him in the name of the people of England, exhibited to them, being a Court constituted by the supreme authority of England, his refusal three several days and times to own them as a Court or to answer to the matter of his charge, his thrice recorded contumacy, and other his contempts and defaults in the precedent courts. Upon which, the Court then declared, that they might not be wanting to themselves or to the trust reposed in them, and that no man's wilfulness ought to serve him to prevent justice; and that they had therefore thought fit to take the substance of what had passed into their serious consideration, to wit, the charge, and the prisoner's contumacy, and the confession which in law does arise upon that contumacy, the notoriety of the fact charged, and other the circumstances material in the cause. And upon the whole matter had resolved and agreed upon a sentence then ready to be pronounced against the prisoner. But that in regard of his desire to be further heard, they were ready to hear him as to anything material which he would offer to their consideration before the sentence given, relating to the defence of himself concerning the matter charged; and did then signify so much to the prisoner; who made use of that leave given only to protest his respects to the peace of the kingdom and liberty of the subject; and to say, That the same made him at last to desire, that having somewhat to say that concerned both, he might before the sentence given be heard in the Painted Chamber, before the Lords and Commons; saying, it was fit to be heard, if it were reason which he should offer, whereof they were judges.

And pressing that point much, he was forthwith answered by the Court, and told, that that which he had moved was a declining of the jurisdiction of the Court, whereof he had caution frequently before given him; that it sounded to further delay, of which he had been too much guilty; that the Court being founded (as often had been said) upon the authority of the Commons of England, in whom rested the supreme jurisdiction, the motion tended to set up another, or a co-ordinate jurisdiction in derogation of the power whereby the Court sat, and to the manifest delay of their justice. In which regard, he was told, they might forthwith proceed to sentence; yet for his further satisfaction of the entire pleasure and judgment of the Court, upon what he had then said, he was told and accordingly it was declared, that the Court would withdraw half an hour.

The prisoner by command being withdrawn, the Court make their recess into the room called the Court of Wards, considered of the prisoner's motion, and gave the President direction to declare their dissent thereto, and to proceed to the sentence.

The Court being again set, and the prisoner returned, was according to their direction informed that he had in effect received his answer before the Court withdrew, and that their judgment was (as to his motion) the same to him before declared; that, the Court acted, and were judges appointed by the highest authority, and that judges were not to delay no more than to deny justice; that they were good words in the great old Charter of England, *Nulli negabimus, nulli vendemus, nulli differemus Justitiam vel Rectum* [To no one shall we deny, sell, or delay justice or right]; that their duty called upon them to avoid further delays and to proceed to judgment, which was their unanimous resolution.

Unto which the prisoner replied, and insisted upon his former desires, confessing a delay, but that it was important for the peace of the kingdom, and therefore pressed again with much earnestness to be heard before the Lords and Commons. In answer whereto, he was told by the Court that they had fully before considered of his proposal and must give him the same answer to his renewed desires and that they were ready to proceed to sentence if he had

Nulli ... Rectum: From the Magna Carta, a document first produced in 1215 and that came to be seen by some as a foundational statement of the rights and liberties of the English, not least in establishing that kings were not above the law.

nothing more to say. Whereunto he subjoined [that] he had no more to say; but desired that might be entered which he had said.

Hereupon, after some discourse used by the President for vindicating the parliament's justice, explaining the nature of the crimes of which the prisoner stood charged, and for which he was to be condemned; and by way of exhortation to the prisoner to a serious repentance for his high transgressions against God and the people, and to prepare for his eternal condition.

The sentence formerly agreed upon and put down in parchment writing, O Yes being first made for silence, was by the Court's command, solemnly pronounced and given: the tenor whereof follows.

Whereas the Commons of England assembled in parliament have by their late Act, entitled, An Act of the Commons of England assembled in parliament for Erecting of an High Court of Justice for the Trying and Judging of Charles Stuart, king of England, authorized and constituted us an High Court of Justice for the trying and judging of the said Charles Stuart for the crimes and treasons in the said Act mentioned. By virtue whereof, the said Charles Stuart has been three several times convented before this High Court, where, the first day, being Saturday the 20 January in pursuance of the said Act, a charge of high treason and other high crimes, was in the behalf of the people of England exhibited against him and read openly unto him, wherein he was charged, that he the said Charles Stuart, being admitted king of England and therein trusted with a limited power, to govern by and according to the law of the land and not otherwise; and by his trust, oath, and office, being obliged to use the power committed to him for the good and benefit of the people and for the preservation of their rights and liberties. Yet nevertheless, out of a wicked design to erect and uphold in himself an unlimited and tyrannical power to rule according to his will, and to overthrow the rights and liberties of the people, and to take away and make void the foundations thereof, and of all redress and remedy of misgovernment, which by the fundamental constitutions of this kingdom were reserved on the people's behalf, in the right and power of frequent and successive parliaments, or national meetings in council, he, the said Charles Stuart, for accomplishment of such his designs and for the protecting of himself and his adherents in his and their wicked practices, to the same end has traitorously and maliciously levied war against the present parliament and people therein represented, as with the circumstances of time and place, is in the said charge more particularly set forth. And that he has thereby caused and procured many thousands of the free people of this nation to be slain; and by divisions, parties, and insurrections within this land, by invasions from foreign parts endeavoured and procured by him, and by many other evil ways and means, he the said Charles Stuart has not only maintained and carried on the said war both by sea and land, but also has renewed or caused to be renewed the said war against the parliament and good people of this nation in this present year

1648[–49], in several counties and places in this kingdom in the charge specified; and that he has for that purpose given his commission to his son the prince, and others, whereby besides multitudes of other persons, many, such as were by the parliament intrusted and employed for the safety of this nation, being by him or his agents corrupted to the betraying of their trust and revolting from the parliament, have had entertainment and commission for the continuing and renewing of the war and hostility against the said parliament and people. And that by the said cruel and unnatural war so levied, continued, and renewed, much innocent blood of the free people of this nation has been spilt, many families undone, the public treasure wasted, trade obstructed and miserably decayed, vast expense and damage to the nation incurred, and many parts of the land spoiled, some of them even to desolation; and that he still continues his commission to his said son and other rebels and revolters, both English and foreigners, and to the Earl of Ormond and to the Irish rebels and revolters associated with him, from whom further invasions upon this land are threatened by his procurement, and on his behalf. And that all the said wicked designs, wars, and evil practices of him the said Charles Stuart were still carried on for the advancement and upholding of the personal interest of will, power and pretended prerogative to himself and his family, against the public interest, common right, liberty, justice and peace of the people of this nation. And that he thereby has been and is the occasioner, author, and continuer of the said unnatural, cruel, and bloody wars, and therein guilty of all the treasons, murders, rapines, burnings, spoils, desolations, damage, and mischief to this nation, acted and committed in the said wars or occasioned thereby. Whereupon, the proceedings and judgment of this Court were prayed against him, as a tyrant, traitor, and murderer, and public enemy to the Commonwealth, as by the said charge more fully appears. To which charge being read unto him as aforesaid, he the said Charles Stuart was required to give his answer; but he refused so to do. And upon Monday, January 22, being again brought before this Court and there required to answer directly to the said charge, he still refused so to do; whereupon his default and contumacy was entered. And the next day, being the third time brought before the Court, judgment was then prayed against him on the behalf of the people of England, for his contumacy and for the matters contained against him in the said charge, as taking the same for confessed in regard of his refusing to answer thereto. Yet notwithstanding, this Court (not willing to take advantage of his contempt) did once more require him to answer to the said charge, but he again refused so to do. Upon which his several defaults, this Court might justly have proceeded to judgment against him, both for his contumacy and the matters of the charge, taking the same for confessed, as aforesaid. Yet nevertheless, this Court for their own clearer information and further satisfaction have thought fit to examine witnesses upon oath and take notice of other evidences touching the matters contained in the said charge, which accordingly they have done.

Now therefore upon serious and mature deliberation of the premises, and consideration had of the notoriety of the matters of fact charged upon him as aforesaid, this Court is in judgment and conscience satisfied that he the said Charles Stuart is guilty of levying war against the said parliament and people and maintaining and continuing the same. For which in the said charge he stands accused, and by the general course of his government, counsels, and practices before and since this parliament began (which have been, and are notorious and public, and the effects whereof remain abundantly upon record) this Court is fully satisfied in their judgments and consciences, that he has been and is guilty of the wicked designs and endeavours in the said charge set forth, and that the said war has been levied, maintained, and continued by him as aforesaid, in prosecution and for accomplishment of the said designs; and that he has been and is the occasioner, author, and continuer of the said unnatural, cruel, and bloody wars, and therein guilty of high treason and of the murders, rapines, burnings, spoils, desolations, damage, and mischief to this nation, acted and committed in the said war and occasioned thereby. For all which treasons and crimes, this Court does adjudge, that he the said Charles Stuart, as a tyrant, traitor, murderer, and public enemy to the good people of this nation, shall be put to death by the severing of his head from his body.

This sentence being read, the President spoke as follows: The sentence now read and published is the act, sentence, judgment, and resolution of the whole Court.

Whereupon the whole Court stood up and owned it.

The prisoner being withdrawn, the Court adjourned itself forthwith into the Painted Chamber. The Court being sat in the Painted Chamber, according to adjournment from Westminster Hall aforesaid; Sir Hardress Waller, Col. Harrison, Commissary Gen. Ireton, Col. Deane, and Col. Okey are appointed to consider of the time and place for the execution of the sentence against the king. And then the Court adjourned itself till Monday morning at eight o'clock to this place.

**[Nalson's inserted text from Mabbott is between the asterisks, with his own edits in italics.]

The more full account of this day's action, take as follows:
The king being come in in his wonted posture, with his hat on, some of the soldiers began to call for justice, justice, and execution. But silence being commanded, His Majesty began: I desire a word, to be heard a little; and I hope I shall give no occasion of interruption.
Bradshaw saucily answered, You may answer in your time; hear the Court first.

His Majesty patiently replied, If it please you, Sir, I desire to be heard; and I shall not give any occasion of interruption; and it is only in a word. A sudden judgment—

Bradshaw: Sir, you shall be heard in due time; but you are to hear the Court first.

King: Sir, I desire it; it will be in order to what I believe the Court will say: and therefore, Sir, a hasty judgment is not so soon recalled.

Bradshaw: Sir, you shall be heard before the judgment be given; and in the meantime you may forbear.

King: Well, Sir, Shall I be heard before the judgment be given?

Bradshaw: Gentlemen, it is well known to all or most of you here present, that the prisoner at the bar has been several times convented and brought before this Court to make answer to a charge of treason and other high crimes exhibited against him in the name of the people of England. To which charge being required to answer, he has been so far from obeying the commands of the Court, by submitting to their justice, as he began to take upon him to offer reasoning and debate unto the authority of the Court, and to the highest court, that appointed them to try and judge him. But being overruled in that and required to make his answer, he was still pleased to continue contumacious and to refuse to submit to answer.

Hereupon the Court, that they might not be wanting to themselves nor the trust reposed in them, nor that any man's wilfulness prevent justice, they have thought fit to take the matter into their consideration. They have considered of the charge, they have considered of the contumacy, and of that confession which in law does arise upon that contumacy; they have likewise considered of the notoriety of the fact charged upon this prisoner. And upon the whole matter they are resolved, and are agreed upon a sentence to be pronounced against this prisoner. But in respect he does desire to be heard before the sentence be read and pronounced, the Court has resolved that they will hear him.

Yet, Sir, thus much I must tell you beforehand, which you have been minded of at other courts, that if that which you have to say, be to offer any debate concerning the jurisdiction, you are not to be heard in it. You have offered it formerly, and you have struck at the root, that is, the power and supreme authority of the Commons of England; which this Court will not admit a debate of, and which indeed it is an irrational thing in them to do, being a Court that acts upon authority derived from them. But, Sir, if you have anything to say in defence of yourself concerning the matter charged, the Court has given me in command to let you know they will hear you.

King: Since I see that you will not hear anything of debate concerning that which I confess I thought most material for the peace of the kingdom and for the liberty of the subject, I shall waive it; I shall speak nothing to it. But only I must tell you, that this many-a-day all things have been taken away from me, but that which I call dearer to me than my life, which is my conscience and my honour. And if I had a respect to my life more than the peace of the kingdom and the liberty of the subject, certainly I should have made a particular defence for myself; for by that at leastwise I might have delayed an ugly sentence, which I believe will pass upon me. Therefore certainly, Sir, as a man that has some understanding, some knowledge of the world, if that my true zeal to my country had not overborn the care that I have for my own preservation, I should have gone another way to work than that I have done. Now, Sir, I conceive that a hasty sentence once past may sooner be repented of than recalled: And truly, the self same desire that I have for the peace of the kingdom and the liberty of the subject, more than my own particular ends, makes me now at last desire that I having something to say that concerns both, before sentence be given, that I may be heard in the Painted Chamber before the Lords and Commons. This delay cannot be prejudicial unto you, whatsoever I say. If that I say no reason, those that hear me must be judges; I cannot be judge of that that I have. If it be reason, and really for the welfare of the kingdom and the liberty of the subject, I am sure on it, it is very well worth the hearing. Therefore I do conjure you, as you love that that you pretend (I hope it is real), the liberty of the subject, the peace of the kingdom, that you will grant me this hearing before any sentence be past. I only desire this, that you will take this into your consideration; it may be you have not heard of it beforehand. If you will, I will retire, and you may think of it: but if I cannot get this liberty, I do protest, that these fair shows of liberty and peace are pure shows, and that you will not hear your king.

Bradshaw: Sir, you have now spoken.

King: Yes, Sir.

Bradshaw: And this that you have said, is a further declining of the jurisdiction of this Court, which was the thing wherein you were limited before.

King: Pray excuse me, Sir, for my interruption, because you mistake me. It is not a declining of it; you do judge me before you hear me speak. I say it will not, I do not decline it; though I cannot acknowledge the jurisdiction of the Court, yet, Sir, in this, give me leave to say, I would do it, though I did not acknowledge it. In this I do protest, it is not the declining of it, since, I say, if that I do say anything but that that is for the peace of the kingdom, and the liberty of the subject, then the shame is mine. Now I desire that you will take this into your consideration: if you will, I will withdraw.

Bradshaw: Sir, this is not altogether new that you have moved to us, not altogether new to us, though the first time in person you have offered it to the Court. Sir, you say you do not decline the jurisdiction of the Court.

King: Not in this that I have said.

Bradshaw: I understand you well, Sir; but nevertheless, that which you have offered seems to be contrary to that saying of yours; for the Court are ready to give a sentence. It is not as you say, that they will not hear their king; for they have been ready to hear you; they have patiently waited your pleasure for three courts together, to hear what you would say to the people's charge against you. To which you have not vouchsafed to give any answer at all. Sir, this tends to a further delay. Truly, Sir, such delays as these, neither may the kingdom nor justice well bear. You have had three several days to have offered in this kind what you would have pleased. This Court is founded upon that authority of the commons of England, in whom rests the supreme jurisdiction. That which you now tender, is to have another jurisdiction and a co-ordinate jurisdiction. I know very well you express yourself, Sir, that notwithstanding that you would offer to the Lords and Commons in the Painted Chamber, yet nevertheless you would proceed on here; I did hear you say so. But, Sir, that you would offer there, whatever it is, must needs be in delay of the justice here. So as if this Court be resolved and prepared for the sentence, this that you offer they are not bound to grant. But, Sir, according to that you seem to desire, and because you shall know the further pleasure of the Court upon that which you have moved, the Court will withdraw for a time.

This he did to prevent the disturbance of their scene by one of their own members, Col. John Downes, who could not stifle the reluctance of his conscience when he saw His Majesty press so earnestly for a short hearing; but declaring himself unsatisfied, forced them to yield to the king's request.

King: Shall I withdraw?

Bradshaw: Sir, you shall know the pleasure of the Court presently.

The Court withdraws for half an hour into the Court of Wards. The Court gives command that the prisoner be withdrawn; and they give order for his return again. *Then withdrawing into the chamber of the Court of Wards, their business was not to consider of His Majesty's desire but to chide Downes, and with reproaches and threats to harden him to go through the remainder of their villainy with them. Which done, they return; and being sat,* Bradshaw commanded, Sergeant at Arms, send for your prisoner. Who being come, Bradshaw proceeded.

Sir, you were pleased to make a motion here to the Court, to offer a desire of yours touching the propounding of somewhat to the Lords and Commons in the Painted Chamber, for the peace of the Kingdom. Sir, you did in effect receive an answer before the Court adjourned: Truly, Sir, their withdrawing and adjournment was *pro forma tantum* [a formality]; for it did not seem to them that there was any difficulty in the thing. They have considered of what you have moved and have considered of their own authority, which is founded, as has been often said, upon the supreme authority of the Commons of England assembled in parliament. The Court acts accordingly to their commission. Sir, the return I have to you from the Court is this, that they have been too much delayed by you already, and this that you now offer has occasioned some little further delay; and they are judges appointed by the highest authority, and judges are no more to delay than they are to deny justice. They are good words in the Great Old Charter of England, *Nulli negabimus, nulli vendemus, nulli deferemus justitiam* [To no one will we deny, sell, or delay justice (Magna Carta)]. There must be no delay. But the truth is, Sir, and so every man here observes it, that you have much delayed them in your contempt and default, for which they might long since have proceeded to judgment against you; and notwithstanding what you have offered, they are resolved to proceed to sentence and to judgment, and that is their unanimous resolution.

King: Sir, I know it is in vain for me to dispute; I am no sceptic for to deny the power that you have; I know that you have power enough. Sir, I must confess, I think it would have been for the kingdom's peace, if you would have taken the pains to have shown the lawfulness of your power. For this delay that I have desired, I confess it is a delay; but it is a delay very important for the peace of the kingdom. For it is not my person that I look at alone, it is the kingdom's welfare and the kingdom's peace.

It is an old sentence, that we should think on long before we resolve of great matters suddenly. Therefore, Sir, I do say again, that I do put at your doors all the inconveniency of a hasty sentence. I confess I have been here now, I think, this week, this day eight days was the day I came here first; but a little delay of a day or two further may give peace, whereas a hasty judgment may bring on that trouble and perpetual inconveniency to the kingdom that the child that is unborn may repent it. And therefore again, out of the duty I owe to God and to my country, I do desire that I may be heard by the Lords and Commons in the Painted Chamber, or any other Chamber that you will appoint me.

Bradshaw: You have been already answered to what you even now moved, being the same you moved before, since the resolution and the judgment of the Court in it. And the Court now requires to know whether you have any more to say for yourself than you have said, before they proceed to sentence.

King: I say this, Sir, that if you hear me, if you will give me but this delay, I doubt not but I shall give some satisfaction to you all here, and to my people after that. And therefore I do require you, as you will answer it at the dreadful day of judgment, that you will consider it once again.

Bradshaw: Sir, I have received direction from the Court.

King: Well, Sir.

Bradshaw: If this must be reinforced, or anything of this nature, your answer must be the same; and they will proceed to sentence, if you have nothing more to say.

King: I have nothing more to say; but I shall desire that this may be entered what I have said.

Bradshaw: The Court then, Sir, has something to say unto you, which although I know it will be very unacceptable, yet notwithstanding they are willing and are resolved to discharge their duty.

Then Bradshaw went on in a long harangue, endeavouring to justify their proceedings, misapplying law and history and raking up and wresting whatsoever he thought fit for his purpose, alleging the examples of former treasons and rebellions, both at home and abroad, as authentic proofs; and concluding that the king was a tyrant, traitor, murderer, and public enemy to the Commonwealth of England.[3] His Majesty having with his wonted patience heard all these reproaches, answered, I would desire only one word before you give sentence, and that is, that you would hear me concerning those great imputations that you have laid to my charge.

Bradshaw: Sir, you must give me now leave to go on; for I am not far from your sentence, and your time is now past.

King: But I shall desire you will hear me a few words to you; for, truly, whatever sentence you will put upon me, in respect of those heavy imputations that I see by your speech you have put upon me. Sir, it is very true that——

---

3   This passage is Nalson's brief summary and dismissal of Mabbott's account of a set-piece speech by Bradshaw; it is included here on p. 79.

Bradshaw: Sir, I must put you in mind: truly, Sir, I would not willingly, at this time especially, interrupt you in anything you have to say that is proper for us to admit of. But, Sir, you have not owned us as a Court, and you look upon us as a sort of people met together, and we know what language we receive from your party.

King: I know nothing of that.

Bradshaw: You disavow us as a Court, and therefore for you to address yourself to us, not to acknowledge us as a Court to judge of what you say, it is not to be permitted. And the truth is, all along from the first time you were pleased to disavow and disown us, the Court needed not to have heard you one word. For unless they be acknowledged a Court, and engaged, it is not proper for you to speak. Sir, we have given you too much liberty already, and admitted of too much delay, and we may not admit of any further. Were it proper for us to do, we should hear you freely, and we should not have declined to have heard you at large, what you could have said or proved on your behalf, whether for totally excusing, or for in part excusing those great and heinous charges that in whole or in part are laid upon you. But, Sir, I shall trouble you no longer; your sins are of so large a dimension, that if you do but seriously think of them, they will drive you to a sad consideration, and they may improve in you a sad and serious repentance. And that the Court doth heartily wish that you may be so penitent for what you have done amiss, that God may have mercy at least wise upon your better part. Truly, Sir, for the other, it is our parts and duties to do that that the law prescribes. We are not here *Jus dare*, but *Jus dicere*. [We are not here to create the law, but to declare it.] We cannot be unmindful of what the Scripture tells us; for to acquit the guilty is of equal abomination as to condemn the innocent. We may not acquit the guilty. What sentence the law affirms to a traitor, [a] tyrant, a murderer, and a public enemy to the country, that sentence you are now to hear read unto you; and that is the sentence of the Court.

Make an O Yes, and command silence while the sentence is read. Which done, their clerk, Broughton, read the sentence, drawn up in parchment.

Whereas the Commons of England in parliament, had appointed them an High Court of Justice for the trial of Charles Stuart, king of England, before whom he had been three times convented, and at the first time a charge of high treason, and other crimes and misdemeanours, was read in the behalf of the kingdom of England. (Here the charge was repeated.) Which charge being read unto him as aforesaid, he the said Charles Stuart was required to give his answer; but he refused so to do.(Expressing the several passages of his refusing in the former Proceedings.)

For all which treasons and crimes, this Court does adjudge, that he the said Charles Stuart as a tyrant, traitor, murderer, and a public enemy, shall be put to death by the severing of his head from his body. Which being read, Bradshaw added, The sentence now read and published is the act, sentence, judgment, and resolution of the whole Court. To which they all expressed their assent by standing up, as was before agreed and ordered.

His Majesty then said, Will you hear me a word, Sir?

Bradshaw: Sir, You are not to be heard after the sentence.

King: No, Sir?

Bradshaw: No, Sir; by your favour, Sir. Guard, withdraw your prisoner.

King: I may speak after sentence, by your favour, Sir, I may speak after sentence, ever.

By your favour, hold: the sentence, Sir,—I say, Sir, I do—I am not suffered to speak; expect what justice other people will have.

His Majesty being taken away by the guard, as he passed down the stairs, the insolent soldiers scoffed at him, casting the smoke of their tobacco (a thing very distasteful unto him) in his face and throwing their pipes in his way. And one more insolent than the rest, spitting in his face, his Majesty, according to his wonted heroic patience, took no more notice of so strange and barbarous an indignity, than to wipe it off with his handkerchief. As he passed along, hearing the rabble of soldiers, crying out, Justice, Justice; he said, Poor Souls, for a piece of money they would do so for their commanders.

Being brought first to Sir Robert Cotton's, and thence to Whitehall, the soldiers continued their brutish carriage toward him, abusing all that seemed to show any respect or even pity to him; not suffering him to rest in his chamber, but thrusting in and smoking their tobacco, and disturbing his privacy. But through all these trials (unusual to princes) he passed with such a calm and even temper, that he let fall nothing unbeseeming his former majesty and magnanimity.

In the evening, a member of the army acquainted the committee with his majesty's desire, that seeing they had passed a sentence of death upon him and his time might be nigh, he might see his children and [that] Doctor Juxon, Bishop of London, might be admitted to assist him in his private devotions and receiving the sacrament. Both which at length were granted.

And the next day, being Sunday, he was attended by the Guard to St. James's, where the bishop preached upon these words, "In the day when God shall judge the secrets of all men by Jesus Christ according to my Gospel."

His Majesty's Speech to the Lady Elizabeth and Henry Duke of Gloucester, January 29, 1649.[4]

Of His Majesty's discourse to his children, there being several relations, it is thought fit to represent the several copies.

I. A true relation of the king's speech to the Lady Elizabeth and the Duke of Gloucester, the day before his death.
His children being come to meet him, he first gave his blessing to the Lady Elizabeth; and bade her remember to tell her brother James, whenever she should see him, that it was his father's last desire, that he should no more look upon Charles as his eldest brother only, but be obedient unto him as his sovereign, and that they should love one another and forgive their father's enemies. Then said the king to her, Sweetheart, you will forget this. No, said she, I shall never forget it whilst I live; and pouring forth abundance of tears, promised him to write down the particulars.

Then the king taking the Duke of Gloucester upon his knee, said, Sweetheart, now they will cut off thy father's head (upon which words, the child looked very steadfastly upon him). Mark, child, what I say; They will cut off my head, and perhaps make thee a king. But mark what I say, you must not be a king so long as your brothers Charles and James do live; for they will cut off your brothers' heads (when they can catch them) and cut off thy head too at last; and therefore I charge you, do not be made a king by them. At which, the child sighing, said, I will be torn in pieces first. Which falling so unexpectedly from one so young, it made the king rejoice exceedingly.

II. Another relation from the Lady Elizabeth's own hand.
What the king said to me the 29th of January 1649. Being the last time I had the happiness to see him, he told me, he was glad I was come; and although he had not time to say much, yet somewhat he had to say to me, which he had not to another, or leave in writing, because he feared their cruelty was such, as that they would not have permitted him to write to me. He wished me not to grieve and torment myself for him, for that would be a glorious death that he should die, it being for the laws and liberties of this land, and for maintaining the true protestant religion. He bid me read Bishop Andrews's Sermons, Hooker's Ecclesiastical Polity, and Bishop Laud's book against Fisher; which would ground me against popery. He told me, he had forgiven all his enemies, and hoped God would forgive them also; and commanded us, and all the rest of my brothers and sisters to forgive them. He bid me tell my mother, that his

---

4   This section obviously constitutes one of Nalson's additions to the original trial record produced by Phelps. The Lady Elizabeth and Henry, Duke of Gloucester were two of Charles's younger children, then aged 13 and 8. Charles had left them behind when he fled the capital in January of 1642, as did his wife Henrietta Maria when she left to secure aid from the Continent, so they had spent years under parliamentary guardianship. Elizabeth would die of pneumonia the year following; Henry was soon thereafter allowed to go to his family on the Continent and survived until just shortly after the Restoration, dying in London in September 1660 from smallpox.

thoughts had never strayed from her, and that his love should be the same to the last. Withal he commanded me and my brother to be obedient to her, and bid me send his blessing to the rest of my brothers and sisters, with commendation to all his friends.

So after he had given me his blessing, I took my leave.

Further, he commanded us all to forgive those people, but never to trust them, for they had been most false to him, and to those that gave them power; and he feared also to their own souls. And desired me not to grieve for him, for he should die a martyr and that he doubted not but the Lord would settle his throne upon his son, and that we should be all happier than we could have expected to have been if he had lived. With many other things, which at present I cannot remember.

III. Another relation from the Lady Elizabeth.

The king said to the Duke of Gloucester, that he would say nothing to him but what was for the good of his soul. He told him, that he heard the Army intended to make him king; but it was a thing not for him to take upon him, if he regarded the welfare of his soul, for he had two brothers before him; and therefore commanded him upon his blessing never to accept of it, unless it redounded lawfully upon him; and commanded him to fear the Lord, and he would provide for him.**

Painted Chamber. Monday, 29 January 1649.

Three proclamations made. The Court is called.

Upon report made from the committee for considering the time and place of the executing of the judgment against the king, that the said committee have resolved, that the open street before Whitehall is a fit place, and that the said committee conceive it fit that the king be there executed the morrow, the king having already notice thereof. The Court approved thereof, and ordered a warrant to be drawn for that purpose; which said warrant was accordingly drawn and agreed unto, and ordered to be engrossed; which was done, and signed and sealed accordingly, as follows, *viz.*

At the High Court of Justice for the trying and judging of Charles Stuart, king of England, Jan. 29, 1649:

Whereas Charles Stuart, king of England, is and stands convicted, attainted, and condemned of high treason and other high crimes, and sentence upon Saturday last was pronounced against him by this Court, to be put to death by the severing of his head from his body, of which sentence, execution yet remains to be done. These are therefore to will and require you to see the said sentence executed in the open street before Whitehall, upon the morrow, being the thirtieth day of this instant month of January, between the hours of ten in the morning, and five in the afternoon of the same day, with full effect. And for so doing, this shall be your sufficient warrant. And these are to require all officers, soldiers, and others, the good people of this nation of England, to be assisting unto you in this service.

Given under our hands and seals. To Col. Francis Hacker, Col. Huncks, and Lieutenant Col. Phray, and to every of them.

[Lists names of the 59 signatories, using red ink.]

It was ordered that the officers of the ordnance within the Tower of London, or any other officer or officers of the store within the said Tower, in whose hands or custody the bright execution axe for the executing malefactors is, do forthwith deliver unto Edward Dendy, esq., sergeant at arms, attending this Court, or his deputy or deputies, the said axe; and for their or either of their so doing, this shall be their warrant. Directed to Col. John White, or any other officer within the Tower of London whom it concerns.

The Court adjourned till tomorrow morning at nine o'clock.

Tuesday, 30 January 1649.
Painted Chamber, Commissioners meet.

Ordered, that Mr. Marshall, Mr. Nye, Mr. Caryl, Mr. Salway, and Mr. Dell be desired to attend the king, to administer to him those spiritual helps as should be suitable to his present condition. And Lieut. Col. Goffe is desired forthwith to repair unto them for that purpose.

Who did so, but after informed the Court, that the king being acquainted therewith, refused to confer with them, expressing that he would not be troubled with them.

Ordered, that the scaffold upon which the king is to be executed be covered with black.

The warrant for executing the king, being accordingly delivered to those parties to whom the same was directed, execution was done upon him, according to the tenor of the said warrant, about two o'clock in the afternoon of the said 30 January.

**[Nalson's interpolation, which seems to draw upon material in the anonymous pamphlet published soon after the king's execution: *King Charles His Speech Made Upon the Scaffold* (London, 1649).]

Mr. Phelps makes as short work of this part of the narrative as his infamous masters had done of their pretended trial of this illustrious innocent. And therefore to supply that defect, take the following account of the conclusion of this dismal tragedy.

Tuesday, 30 January, the fatal day being come, the commissioners met and ordered four or five of their ministers to attend upon the king at St. James's, where they then kept him. But his Majesty well knowing what miserable comforters they were like to prove, refused to have conference with them. That morning, before his Majesty was brought thence, the Bishop of London (who with much ado was permitted to wait upon him a day or two before, and to assist him in that sad instant) read divine service in his presence; in which the 27th. of St. Matthew (the history of our Saviour's crucifixion) proved the second lesson. The king supposing it to have been selected on purpose, thanked him afterwards for his seasonable choice. But the bishop modestly declining that undue thanks, told him that it was the lesson appointed by the calendar for that day. He also then and there received of the bishop the Holy Sacrament, and performed all his devotions in preparation to his Passion.

Which ended, about ten o'clock his Majesty was brought from St. James's to Whitehall by a regiment of foot, with colours flying and drums beating, part marching before, and part behind, with a private guard of partisans about him, the bishop on the one hand, and Col. Tomlinson (who had the charge of him) on the other, both bare-headed, his Majesty walking very fast, and bidding them go faster, added, that he now went before them to strive for an heavenly crown, with less solicitude than he had often encouraged his soldiers to fight for an earthly diadem.

Being come to the end of the park, he went up the stairs leading to the Long Gallery in Whitehall and so into the Cabinet Chamber, where he used formerly to lodge. There finding an unexpected delay in being brought upon the scaffold, which they had not as then fitted, he passed the time, at convenient distances, in prayer.

About twelve o'clock, his Majesty refusing to dine, only ate a bit of bread and drank a glass of claret. And about an hour after, Col. Hacker, with other officers and soldiers, brought him, with the bishop and Col. Tomlinson, through the Banqueting House to the scaffold, to which the passage was made through a window. Divers companies of foot and troops of horse were placed on each side of the street, which hindered the approach of the very numerous spectators, and the king from speaking what he had premeditated and prepared for them to hear. Whereupon, his Majesty finding himself disappointed, omitted much of his intended matter; and for what he meant to speak, directed himself chiefly to Col. Tomlinson. […] Then turning to the officers, he said, Sirs, Excuse me for this same, I have a good cause, and I have a gracious God, I will say no more.

Then to Col. Hacker he said, Take care that they do not put me to pain. And, Sir, this, and it please you—

But a gentleman coming near the axe, the king said, Take heed of the axe, pray take heed of the axe.

And to the executioner he said, I shall say but very short prayers, and when I thrust out my hands—

Then he called to the bishop for his cap, and having put it on asked the executioner, Does my hair trouble you? Who desired him to put it all under his cap; which as he was doing, by the help of the bishop and the executioner, he turned to the bishop, and said, I have a good cause and a gracious God on my side. The bishop said, There is but one stage more; which, though turbulent and troublesome, yet it is a very short one. You may consider it will soon carry you a very great way; it will carry you from Earth to Heaven; and there you shall find, to your great joy, the prize you hasten to, a crown of glory. The king adjoins, I go from a corruptible to an incorruptible crown, where no disturbance can be, no disturbance in the world.

Bishop: You are exchanged from a temporal to an eternal crown. A good exchange!

Then the king asked the executioner, Is my hair well? And taking off his cloak and **George**, he delivered his George to the Bishop, saying, Remember. Then putting off his doublet, and being in his waistcoat, he put on his cloak again, and looking upon the block, said to the executioner, You must set it fast.

Executioner: It is fast, Sir.

King: It might have been a little higher.

Executioner: It can be no higher, Sir.

King: When I put out my hands this way, then——

Then having said a few words to himself, as he stood, with hands and eyes lift up, immediately stooping down, he laid his neck upon the block, and the executioner again putting his hair under his cap, his Majesty thinking he had been going to strike bade, Stay for the sign.

Executioner: Yes I will and it please your Majesty.

After a very short pause, his Majesty stretching forth his hands, the executioner severed his head from his body: Which being held up and showed to the people, was with his body put into a coffin covered with velvet and carried into his lodging.

His blood was taken up by divers persons for different ends: By some as trophies of their villainy, by others as relics of a martyr; and in some has had the same effect by the blessing of God, which was often found in his sacred touch when living. […]**

George: Insignia of the Order of the Garter, depicting the patron saint of England, St. George.

DOCUMENT 2:

Lord President Bradshaw's Speech: Extract from Gilbert Mabbott,
A Perfect Narrative of the Whole Proceedings of the High Court of Justice
(London, 1649)

That the account given by Nalson is not entirely a "true copy" from his sources
is shown in his decision to paraphrase and dismiss the key speech given by Lord
President Bradshaw on 27 January, a speech included in the publication by reporter
Gilbert Mabbott that Nalson otherwise relied on to supplement Phelps's roll.
As this sets out some of the key historical arguments used to justify the trial and
execution of the king, it is included here.

ev

Lord President: The Court then, Sir, has something else to say unto you,
which although I know it will be very unacceptable, yet notwithstanding
they are willing, and are resolved to discharge their duty.

Sir, you spoke very well of a precious thing that you call peace, and it had
been much to be wished that God had put it into your heart that you had as
effectually and really endeavoured and studied the peace of the kingdom as
now in words you seem to pretend. But as you were told the other day, actions
must expound intentions, yet actions have been clean contrary. And truly Sir, it
doth appear plainly enough to them, that you have gone upon very erroneous
principles, the kingdom has felt it to their smart, and it will be no ease to you
to think of it, for Sir, you have held yourself and let fall such language as if you
had been no ways subject to the law, or that the law had not been your superior.
Sir, the Court is very well sensible of it, and I hope so are all the understanding
people of England, that the law is your superior, that you ought to have ruled
according to the law, you ought to have done so.

Sir, I know very well your pretence has been that you have done so, but Sir,
the difference has been who shall be the expositors of this law, Sir, whether
you and your party out of courts of justice shall take upon them to expound
law, or the courts of justice, who are the expounders; nay, the sovereign and the
High Court of Justice, the parliament of England, that are not only the highest
expounders, but the sole makers of the law. Sir, for you to set yourself with your
single judgment, and those that adhere unto you, to set yourself against the
highest court of justice, that is not law. Sir, as the law is your superior, so truly
Sir, there is something that is superior to the law, and that is indeed the parent
or author of the law, and that is the people of England. For, Sir, as they are
those that at the first (as other countries have done) did choose to themselves
this form of government, even for justice's sake, that justice might be adminis-
tered, that peace might be preserved; so Sir, they gave laws to their governors,

according to which they should govern. And if those laws should have proved inconvenient or prejudicial to the public, they had a power in them and reserved to themselves to alter as they shall see cause. Sir, it is very true, what some of your side have said, *Rex non habet parem in regno* [the king has no peer in the realm]. This Court will say the same, while king, that you have not your peer in some sense, for you are ***major singulis***, but they will aver again, that you are ***minor universis***. And the same author tells you, that in ***exhibitione juris***, there you have no power, but ***in quasi minimus***. This we know to be law, ***Rex habet superiorem, Deum & Legem, etiam & curiam***, and so says the same author. And truly, Sir, he makes bold to go a little further, *Debent ei ponere frenum*, they ought to bridle him.

And Sir, we know very well the stories of old, those wars that were called the **Barons' Wars**, when the nobility of the land did stand out for the liberty and property of the subject and would not suffer the kings that did invade to play the tyrants freely, but called them to account for it. We know that truth, that they did *frenum ponere* [place a bridle on them]. But Sir, if they do forbear to do their duty now, and are not so mindful of their own honour and the kingdom's good as the barons of England of old were, certainly the commons of England will not be unmindful of what is for their preservation, and for their safety, *Justitiae fruendi causâ reges constituti sunt* [justice is the reason kings were made]: this we learn, the end of having kings, or any other governors, it's for the enjoying of justice, that's the end. Now, Sir, if so be the king will go contrary to that end, or any other governor will go contrary to the end of his government, Sir, he must understand that he is but an officer in trust, and he ought to discharge that trust, and they are to take order for the animadversion and punishment of such an offending governor.

This is not law of yesterday, Sir, since the time of the division betwixt you and your people, but it is law of old. And we know very well the authors and the authorities that do tell us what the law was in that point upon the election of kings, upon the oath that they took unto their people; and if they did not observe it, there were those things called parliaments. The parliaments were they that were to adjudge (the very words of the author) the plaints and wrongs done of the king and the queen or their children, such wrongs especially when the people could have nowhere else any remedy. Sir, that has been the people of England's case, they could not have their remedy elsewhere but in parliament.

Sir, parliaments were ordained for that purpose to redress the grievances of the people, that was their main end. And truly, Sir, if so be that the kings of England had been rightly mindful of themselves, they were never more in majesty and state than in the parliament: but how forgetful some have been, stories have told us. We have a miserable, a lamentable, a sad experience of it. Sir, by the old laws of England, I speak these things the rather to you, because you

---

major singulis ... minor universis: From the thirteenth-century legal treatise by Henry Bracton, *On the Laws and Customs of England*: "rex est major singulis, minor universis," meaning that "the king is greater than each singly, but less than all universally."

exhibitione juris ... in quasi minimus: Again from Bracton, referencing a line that asserts that in the administration of justice, the king ought to have the least power in a case concerning himself.

Rex habet superiorem ... curiam: Again from Bracton: The king has superiors, God and laws and also courts.

Barons' Wars: Referencing two civil wars of the Middle Ages, the First Barons' War (1215–17) against King John, after his repudiation of Magna Carta, and the Second Barons' War (1264–67), against King Henry III, in an attempt to have this king, too, recognize the limits imposed by Magna Carta.

were pleased to let fall the other day, you thought you had as much knowledge in the law as most gentlemen in England; it is very well, Sir. And truly, Sir, it is very fit for the gentlemen of England to understand that law under which they must live, and by which they must be governed. And then Sir, the Scripture says, they that know their masters' will and do it not, what follows? The law is your master, the Acts of parliament.

The parliaments were to be kept anciently we find in our old author twice in the year, that the subject upon any occasion might have a ready remedy and redress for his grievance. Afterwards by several Acts of parliament in the days of your predecessor Edward III, they must have been once a year. Sir, what the intermission of parliament has been in your time it is very well known, and the sad consequences of it, and what in the interim instead of these parliaments had been by you by an high and arbitrary hand introduced upon the people, that likewise has been too well known and felt. But when God by his Providence had so far brought it about, that you could no longer decline the calling of a parliament, Sir, yet it will appear what your ends were against the ancient and your native kingdom of Scotland: The parliament of England not serving your ends against them, you were pleased to dissolve it. Another great necessity occasioned the calling of this parliament, and what your designs and plots and endeavours all along have been for the crushing and confounding of this parliament has been very notorious to the whole kingdom. And truly, Sir, in that you did strike at all, that had been a sure way to have brought about that that this charge lays upon you, your intention to subvert the fundamental laws of the land. For the great bulwark of the liberties of the people is the parliament of England and to subvert and root up that, which your aim has been to do, certainly at one blow you had confounded the liberties and the property of England.

Truly, Sir, it makes me call to mind—I cannot forbear to express it, for Sir, we must deal plainly with you, according to the merits of your cause, so is our commission—it makes me call to mind (these proceedings of yours) that we read of a great Roman emperor, by the way let us call him a great Roman tyrant, Caligula, that wished that the people of Rome had had but one neck, that at one blow he might cut it off. And your proceedings have been somewhat like to this; for the body of the people of England has been (and where else) represented but in the parliament, and could you have but confounded that, you had at one blow cut off the neck of England. But God has reserved better things for us, and has pleased to confound your designs, and to break your forces, and to bring your person into custody that you might be responsible to justice.

Sir, we know very well, that it is a question on your side very much pressed, by what precedent we shall proceed? Truly, Sir, for precedents, I shall not upon these occasions institute any long discourse, but it is no new thing to cite precedents almost of all nations, where the people (when power has been in their hands) have been made bold to call their kings to account, and where the change of government has been upon occasion of the tyranny and mis-government of those that have been placed over them. I will not spend time to mention France, or Spain, or the **Empire**, or other countries; volumes may be written of it. But truly Sir, that of the Kingdom of Aragon, I shall think some of us have thought upon it, when they have the Justice of Aragon, that is a man *tanquam in medio positus* [as if in the middle position], betwixt the king of Spain and the people of the country, that if wrong be done by he that is the king of Aragon, the Justice has power to reform the wrong, and he is acknowledged to be the king's superior, and is the grand preserver of their privileges, and has prosecuted kings upon their miscarriages.

Sir, what the **Tribunes of Rome** were heretofore, and what the **Ephori** were to the Lacedaemonian state we know; that is the parliament of England to the English state. And though Rome seemed to lose its liberty when once the Emperors were, yet you shall find some famous acts of justice even done by the Senate of Rome, that great tyrant of his time Nero, condemned and judged by the Senate. But truly, Sir, to you I should not mention these foreign examples and stories. If you look but over the [River] Tweed, we find enough in your native kingdom of Scotland. If we look to your first King Fergus that your stories make mention of, he was an elective king; he died and left two sons both in their minority, the kingdom made choice of their uncle his brother to govern in the minority. Afterwards the elder brother giving small hopes to the people that he would rule or govern well, seeking to supplant that good uncle of his that governed then justly, they set the elder aside, and took to the younger.

Sir, if I should come to what your stories make mention of, you know very well you are the 109th king of Scotland; for to mention so many kings as that kingdom, according to their power and privilege, have made bold to deal withal, some to banish, and some to imprison, and some to put to death, it would be too long. And as one of your own authors says, it would be too long to recite the manifold examples that your own stories make mention of; *reges* (say they) we do create, we created kings at first; *leges,* &c. we imposed laws upon them.[1] And as they are chosen by the suffrages [i.e., elections] of the people at the first, so, upon just occasion, by the same suffrages they may be taken down again. And we will be bold to say, that no kingdom has yielded more plentiful experience than that your native kingdom of Scotland has done concerning the deposition and the punishment of their offending and transgressing kings, &c.

It is not far to go for an example near you, your **grandmother** set aside, and your father as infant crowned. And the state did it here in England; here has not been a want of some examples, they have made bold (the parliament, and the people of England) to call their kings to account. There are frequent

---

1 Probably referencing George Buchanan, *De Jure Regni apud Scotos* [The Powers of the Crown in Scotland], written in 1579 and explaining the limits within which kings operated, produced after the forced abdication of Mary, Queen of Scots.

examples of it in the Saxons' time, the time before the Conquest [of 1066]. Since the Conquest there want not some precedents neither; King Edward II, King Richard II were dealt with so by the parliament, as they were deposed and deprived. And truly Sir, whoever shall look into their stories, they shall not find the articles that are charged upon them to come near to that height and capitalness of crimes that are laid to your charge, nothing near.

Sir, you were pleased to say the other day wherein they dissent, and I did not contradict it, but take altogether, Sir, if you were as the charge speaks, and no otherwise admitted king of England but for that you were pleased then to allege, now that almost for a thousand years these things have been, stories will tell you, if you go no higher than the time of the Conquest, if you do come down since the Conquest, you are the twenty-fourth king from William the Conqueror, you shall find one half of them to come merely from the state, and not merely upon the point of descent. It were easy to be instanced to you; the time must not be lost that way. And truly Sir, what a grave and learned judge in his time and well known to you, and is since printed for posterity, that although there was such a thing as a descent many times, yet the kings of England ever held the greatest assurance of their titles when it was declared by parliament. And Sir, your oath, the manner of your coronation doth show plainly, that the kings of England, although it's true by the law the next person in blood is design[at]ed, yet if there were just cause to refuse him, the people of England might do it. For there is a contract and bargain made between the king and his people, and your oath is taken, and certainly Sir, the bond is reciprocal, for as you are the liege lord, so they liege subjects. And we know very well that has been so much spoken of, *ligantia est duplex* [a twofold bond]: this we know now, the one tie, the one bond, is the bond of protection that is due from the sovereign, the other is the bond of subjection that is due from the subject. Sir, if this bond be once broken, farewell sovereignty, **Subjectio trahit**, &c.

These things may not be denied, Sir. I speak it the rather, and I pray God it may work upon your heart, that you may be sensible of your miscarriages. For whether you have been as by your office you ought to be, a protector of England, or the destroyer of England, let all England judge, or all the world that has looked upon it. Sir, though you have it by inheritance in the way that is spoken of, yet it must not be denied that your office was an office of trust, and indeed, an office of the highest trust lodged in any single person. For as you were the grand administrator of justice, and others were as your delegates to see it done throughout your realms, if your great office were to do justice and preserve your people from wrong, and instead of doing that you will be the great wrongdoer yourself; if instead of being a conservator of the peace, you will be the grand disturber of the peace, surely this is contrary to your office, contrary to your trust.

Now Sir, if it be an office of inheritance, as you speak of your title by descent, let all men know that great offices are seizable and forfeitable, as if you had it

Subjectio trahit: Referencing a familiar legal maxim, "Protectio trahit subjectionem et subjectio trahit protectionem," meaning that protection draws with it subjection, and subjection draws with it protection; that is, referencing the notion of a twofold, mutual bond that promises subjection in exchange for protection, and protection in exchange for subjection.

but for a year and for your life. Therefore, Sir, it will concern you to take into your serious consideration your great miscarriages in this kind.

Truly Sir, I shall not particularize the many miscarriages of your reign whatsoever, they are famously known. It had been happy for the kingdom, and happy for you, too, if it had not been so much known and so much felt, as the story of your miscarriages must needs be, and has been already.

Sir, that that we are now upon, by the command of the highest court, has been and is to try and judge you for these great offences of yours. Sir, the charge has called you tyrant, a traitor, a murderer, and a public enemy to the Commonwealth of England. Sir, it had been well, if that any of all these terms might rightly and justly have been spared, if any one of them at all.

King: Ha!

Rex ... opprimit:
Paraphrasing Bracton again, to note that he is a king who rules well but a tyrant when he oppresses the people.

Lord President: Truly Sir, we have been told, **Rex est dum bene regit, tyrannus qui populum opprimit**, and if so be that be the definition of a tyrant, then see how you come short of it in your actions, whether the highest tyrant by that way of arbitrary government, and that you have sought for to introduce, and that you have sought to put, you were putting upon the people, whether that was not as high an act of tyranny as any of your predecessors were guilty of, nay, many degrees beyond it.

Sir, the term traitor cannot be spared. We shall easily agree it must denote and suppose a breach of trust, and it must suppose it to be done by a superior, and therefore Sir, as the people of England might have incurred that respecting you, if they had been truly guilty of it, as to the definition of law, so on the other side, when you did break your trust to the kingdom, you did break your trust to your superior: For the kingdom is that for which you were trusted. And therefore, Sir, for this breach of trust when you are called to account, you are called to account by your superiors. And, Sir, the people of England cannot be so far wanting to themselves, which God having dealt so miraculously and gloriously for, they having power in their hands and their great enemy, they must proceed to do justice to themselves, and to you. For, Sir, the Court could heartily desire, that you would lay your hand upon your heart and consider what you have done amiss, that you would endeavour to make your peace with God. Truly, Sir, these are your high crimes: tyranny and treason.

There is a third thing, too, if those had not been, and that is murder, which is laid to your charge. All the bloody murders that have been committed since this time that the division was betwixt you and your people must be laid to your charge, that have been acted or committed in these late wars. Sir, it is a heinous and crying sin. And truly Sir, if any man will ask us what punishment is due to a murderer, let God's law, let man's law speak. Sir, I will presume that you are so well read in Scripture as to know what God himself has said concerning the shedding of man's blood; **Genesis 9** and **Numbers 35** will tell you what the punishment is, and which this Court in behalf of the kingdom are sensible of, of that innocent blood that has been shed, whereby indeed the land stands still defiled with that blood. And as the text has it, it can no way be cleansed but with the shedding of the blood of him that shed this blood. Sir, we know no dispensation from this blood in that commandment, Thou shalt do no murder. We do not know but that it extends to kings, as well as to the meanest peasants, the meanest of the people. The command is universal. Sir, God's law forbids it, man's law forbids it, nor do we know that there is any manner of exception, not even in man's laws, for the punishment of murder in you. 'Tis true, that in the case of kings, every private hand was not to put forth itself to this work for their reformation and punishment. But, Sir, the people represented having power in their hands, had there been but one wilful act of murder by you committed, had power to have convened you, and to have punished you for it.

But then, Sir, the weight that lies upon you in all those respects that have been spoken, by reason of your tyranny, treason, breach of trust, and the murders that have been committed; surely, Sir, it must drive you into a sad consideration concerning your eternal condition. As I said at first, I know it cannot be pleasing to you to hear any such things as these are mentioned unto you from this Court, for so we do call ourselves and justify ourselves to be a court, and a High Court of Justice, authorized by the highest and solemnest Court of the Kingdom, as we have often said. And although you do yet endeavour what you may to dis-court us, yet we do take knowledge of ourselves to be such a Court as can administer justice to you, and we are bound, Sir, in duty to do it. Sir, all I shall say before the reading of your sentence, it is but this: The Court does heartily desire that you will seriously think of those evils that you stand guilty of. Sir, you said well to us the other day, you wished us to have God before our eyes. Truly, Sir, I hope all of us have so, that God that we know is a King of Kings, and Lord of Lords, that God with whom there is no respect of persons, that God that is the avenger of innocent blood, we have that God before us, that God that does bestow a curse upon them that withhold their hands from shedding of blood, which is in the case of guilty malefactors, and that do deserve death. That God we have before our eyes, and were it not that the conscience of our duty has called us unto this place, and this employment, Sir, you should have had no appearance of a Court here: but Sir, we must prefer the discharge of our duty unto God, and unto the Kingdom, before any other respect whatsoever. And although at this time many of us, if not all of us, are severely threatened by some of your party what they intend to do, Sir, we do here declare, that we shall not decline or forbear the doing of our duty in the administration of justice even to you, according to the merit of your offence, although God should permit those men to effect all that bloody design in hand against us. Sir, we will say, and we will declare it, as those children in the fiery

Genesis 9:6: "Whoso sheds man's blood, by man shall his blood be shed: for in the image of God made he man."

Numbers 35:16–18 insists that "the murderer shall surely be put to death." Verse 33: "… the land cannot be cleansed of the blood that is shed therein, but by the blood of him that shed it."

worship the golden image: Referencing the biblical account in the third chapter of Daniel, of three young Jewish men thrown into a fiery furnace by Nebuchadnezzar, king of Babylon, for their refusal to obey his order to worship an idol, and ultimately protected by God.

Uriah: Referencing the biblical account (2 Samuel 12) of King David, who secured the death of Uriah so that he might marry Uriah's wife, Bathsheba. God ultimately did not demand the repentant David's life, but did take the life of his first child with Bathsheba.

furnace, that would not **worship the golden image** that Nebuchadnezzar had set up, that their God was able to deliver them from that danger that they were near unto. But yet if he would not do it, yet, notwithstanding that, they would not fall down and worship the image: we shall thus apply it, that though we should not be delivered from those bloody hands and hearts that conspire the overthrow of the kingdom in general, of us in particular, for acting in this great work of justice, though we should perish in the work, yet by God's grace, and by God's strength, we will go on with it: And this is all our resolutions.

Sir, I say for yourself, we do heartily wish and desire that God would be pleased to give you a sense of your sins, that you would see wherein you have done amiss, that you may cry unto him, that God would deliver you from blood-guiltiness. A good king was once guilty of that particular thing, and was clear otherwise, saving in the matter of **Uriah**. Truly Sir, the story tells us, that he was a repentant king, and it signifies enough that he had died for it, but that God was pleased to accept of him, and to give him his pardon, "Thou shalt not die, but the child shall die, thou hast given cause to the enemies of God to blaspheme." […]

The Death Warrant of Charles I

Upon passing its sentence of death upon the king, the Court ordered the
production of a warrant addressed to three officers to authorize them to put
the sentence into effect. Engrossed on parchment, it shows signs of erasures
(by scraping away the top layer of skin) and additions, which has led to some
speculation about last-minute changes to the names of the officers charged with
executing the sentence and possible doubts amongst some of the signatories.
Ultimately signed and sealed by 59 individuals, the warrant later served to identify
the "regicides" that the restored House of Lords held most culpable. It remains in
the possession of the House of Lords today. Notice the signatures of Cromwell and
Bradshaw in the first column, and of Harrison in the third.

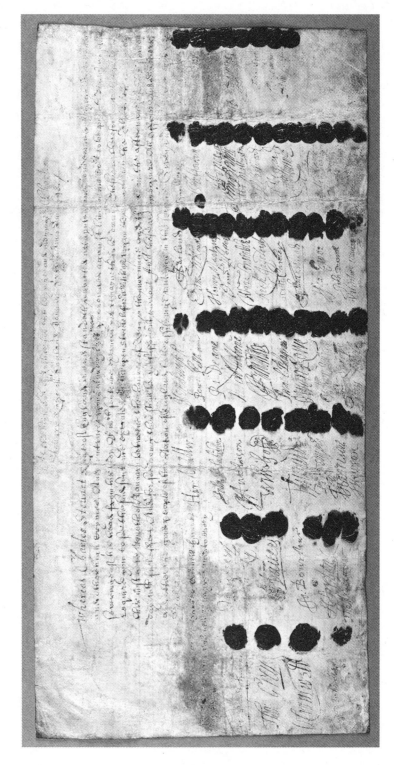

"The Death Warrant of Charles I," The Parliamentary Archives, House of Lords, Westminster, London. Used with permission.

PART 2

PART 2

Reactions and Aftermath

DOCUMENT 4:

Acts Establishing a Republic

With the king dead, what next? Another king, or something different? With these Acts of Parliament, the trimmed version of the body that had once constituted only one of the three entities that made a parliament—the House of Commons— abolished the monarchy, as well as the House of Lords, and established a republican form of government. What do these Acts suggest about the reasons for these decisions and the ways in which their authors sought to justify them?

Significantly, these measures were called Acts at the time. Traditionally, a bill only became an Act of Parliament after both the Commons and Lords agreed and the sovereign gave his or her assent. Measures passed by the House of Lords and House of Commons in the interval between King Charles's flight from the capital and January of 1649, while treated as being of the same statutory force as traditional Acts, were called "ordinances," in deference to the notion that the king's assent was needed to make them law. In January of 1649, however, the Commons claimed for themselves undivided legislative authority and confidently described the measures they passed as Acts. In a vote on 4 January, the Commons declared that "the people are, under God, the original of all just power," adding to it that the Commons, "being chosen by and representing the people, have the supreme power in this nation," and thus, "whatsoever is enacted or declared for law by the Commons, in parliament assembled, has the force of a law, and all the people of this nation are concluded thereby, though the consent and concurrence of the king or House of Peers be not had thereunto." The first such measure was that of 6 January authorizing the king's trial. After the restoration of the monarchy in 1660, all measures that had passed without the assent of the king, whether called ordinances or Acts, were deemed null and void. They do not appear in the official collection of the *Statutes of the Realm*, though in the late nineteenth century the Statute Law Committee did order their compilation as matters of historical interest.

DOCUMENT 4a:

Extracts from "An Act for the abolishing the Kingly Office in England and Ireland, and the Dominions thereunto belonging" (introduced 15 February; passed 17 March 1649)[1]

attainted: In law, the blood of individuals found guilty of high treason was "corrupted," which meant that their children could not inherit through them.

Whereas Charles Stuart, late king of England, Ireland, and the territories and dominions thereunto belonging, has by authority derived from parliament, been, and is hereby declared to be justly condemned, adjudged to die, and put to death, for many treasons, murders, and other heinous offences committed by him, by which judgement he stood and is hereby declared to be **attainted** of high treason, whereby his issue and posterity, and all others pretending title under him, are become incapable of the said Crowns, or of being king or queen of the said kingdom or dominions, or either or any of them; Be it therefore enacted and ordained, and it is enacted, ordained, and declared by this present parliament, and by authority thereof, that all the people of England and Ireland, and the dominions and territories thereunto belonging, of what degree or condition so ever, are discharged of all fealty, homage, and allegiance which is or shall be pretended to be due unto any of the issue and posterity of the said late king, or any claiming under him; and that Charles Stuart, eldest son, and James called Duke of York, second son, and all other the issue and posterity of him the said late king, and all and every person and persons pretending title from, by or under him, are and be disabled to hold or enjoy the said Crown of England and Ireland, and other the dominions thereunto belonging, or any of them; or to have the name, title, style, or dignity of king or queen of England and Ireland, Prince of Wales, or any of them....

Office of a King not to be exercised by any one person.
And whereas it is and has been found by experience, that the office of a king in this nation and Ireland, and to have the power thereof in any single person, is unnecessary, burdensome, and dangerous to the liberty, safety, and public interest of the people, and that for the most part, use has been made of the regal power and prerogative to oppress and impoverish and enslave the subject; and that usually and naturally any one person in such power makes it his interest to encroach upon the just freedom and liberty of the people, and to promote the setting up of their own will and power above the laws, that so they might enslave these kingdoms to their own lust; Be it therefore enacted and ordained by this present parliament, and by authority of the same, that the office of a king in this nation shall not henceforth reside in or be exercised by any one single

1   C.H. Firth and R.S. Rait, ed., *Acts and Ordinances of the Interregnum, 1642–1660* (London: HMSO, 1911), 3 vols, II, 18–20.

person; and that no one person whatsoever shall or may have or hold the office, style, dignity, power, or authority of king of the said kingdoms and dominions, or any of them, or of the Prince of Wales, any law, statute, usage, or custom to the contrary thereof in any wise notwithstanding....

Representatives.

And whereas by the abolition of the kingly office provided for in this Act, a most happy way is made for this nation (if God see it good) to return to its just and ancient right of being governed by its own representatives or national meetings in council, from time to time chosen and entrusted for that purpose by the people, it is therefore resolved and declared by the Commons assembled in parliament, that they will put a period to the sitting of this present parliament, and dissolve the same so soon as may possibly stand with the safety of the people that have entrusted them, and with what is absolutely necessary for the preserving and upholding the government now settled in the way of a Commonwealth; and that they will carefully provide for the certain choosing, meeting, and sitting of the next and future representatives, with such other circumstances of freedom in choice and equality in distribution of members to be elected thereunto, as shall most conduce to the lasting freedom and good of this Commonwealth.

Obedience to the Supreme Authority.

And it is hereby further enacted and declared, notwithstanding anything contained in this Act, no person or persons of what condition and quality so ever, within the Commonwealth of England and Ireland, Dominion of Wales, the Islands of Guernsey and Jersey, and Town of Berwick upon Tweed, shall be discharged from the obedience and subjection which he and they owe to the government of this nation, as it is now declared, but all and every of them shall in all things render and perform the same, as of right is due unto the supreme authority hereby declared to reside in this and the successive representatives of the people of this nation, and in them only.

DOCUMENT 4B:

Extracts from "An Act for the Abolishing the House of Peers"
(introduced 6 February; passed 19 March 1649)[2]

The Commons of England assembled in parliament, finding by too long experience that the House of Lords is useless and dangerous to the people of England to be continued, have thought fit to ordain and enact, and be it

---

2 *Ibid.*, II, 24.

ordained and enacted by this present parliament, and by the authority of the same, that from henceforth the House of Lords in parliament shall be and is hereby wholly abolished and taken away; and that the Lords shall not from henceforth meet or sit in the said House called The Lords House, or in any other house or place whatsoever, as a House of Lords; nor shall sit, vote, advise, adjudge, or determine of any matter or thing whatsoever, as a House of Lords in parliament. Nevertheless it is hereby declared, that neither such Lords as have demeaned themselves with honour, courage, and fidelity to the commonwealth, nor their posterities who shall continue so, shall be excluded from the public councils of the nation, but shall be admitted thereunto, and have their free vote in parliament, if they shall be thereunto elected, as other persons of interest elected and qualified thereunto, ought to have.

DOCUMENT 4C:

"An Act Declaring and Constituting the People of England to be a Commonwealth and Free State" (19 May 1649)[3]

Be it declared and enacted by this present parliament and by the authority of the same, that the people of England, and of all the dominions and territories thereunto belonging, are and shall be, and are hereby constituted, made, established, and confirmed to be a Commonwealth and Free State: And shall from henceforth be governed as a Commonwealth and Free State, by the supreme authority of this nation, the representatives of the people in parliament, and by such as they shall appoint and constitute as officers and ministers under them for the good of the people, and that without any king or House of Lords.

---

3 *Ibid.*, II, 122.

DOCUMENT 5:

A Contemporary Depiction of the King's Execution

News of the king's execution spread far and fast, reaching Russia and even Japan within a year.[1] This print by an unknown engraver was one of many German publications on the topic and exists in several variants, with copies produced in both Frankfurt and Strasbourg now held in the British Library. It most likely drew on published or second-hand accounts rather than any eye-witness experience by the artist. Does the image betray the artist's sympathies? Why might such images have found a ready and widespread market? How might they have shaped reactions to the execution?

---

[1]   Geoffrey Parker, *Global Crisis: War, Climate Change and Catastrophe in the Seventeenth Century* (New Haven: Yale UP, 2013), pp. xvi, 565, 569.

White Hall

BANCKET HAVS.

DOCUMENT 6:

A "Martyr" Speaks from the Grave: The King's *Eikon Basilike*

Extracts from *Eikon Basilike: The Portraiture of His Sacred Majesty in His Solitudes and Sufferings. Together with his Majesty's Prayers Delivered to Doctor Juxon immediately before his death. Also His Majesty's Reasons, against the pretended jurisdiction of the High Court of Justice, which he intended to deliver in Writing on Monday, January 22, 1649* (London, 1649).

Purporting to be the king's own spiritual autobiography, this work appeared immediately after Charles's execution. It subsequently reappeared in about thirty-five editions by year's end and many more in the years that followed—and in a variety of languages and sizes—despite a parliamentary ban on its printing. While Charles may have had a hand in some of its sections, it was almost certainly written by others.[1] A remarkably effective piece of propaganda for the royalist cause, it did much to prepare the way for the restoration of monarchy in 1660 and for later commemorations of Charles as a martyr, with a day for his veneration included in the church calendar from 1660 through to the mid-nineteenth century. The brief selections included here show something of how the text depicted him as Christ-like in his suffering and the rationale presented for his refusal to enter a plea in Court.

To thee (O My God) do I still appeal, whose all discerning justice sees through all the disguises of men's pretensions and deceitful darknesses of their hearts. Thou gave me a heart to grant much to my subjects, and now I need a heart fitted to suffer much from some of them. Thy will be done, though never so much to the crossing of ours, even when we hope to do what might be most conformable to thine and theirs too; who pretended they aimed at nothing else.

Let thy Grace teach me wisely to enjoy as well the frustrating, as the fulfilling of my best hopes and most specious desires. I see while I thought to allay others' fears, I have raised my own; and by settling them, have unsettled myself. Thus have they requited me evil for good, and hatred for my good will towards them. O Lord, be thou my pilot in this dark and dangerous storm, which neither admits my return to the port whence I set out, nor my making any other with that safety and honour which I designed. 'Tis easy for thee to keep me safe in the love and confidence of my people; nor is it hard for thee to preserve me amidst the unjust hatred and jealousies of too many, which thou

---

1   For an examination of disputes over its authorship and purpose, see Sean Kelsey, "The King's Book: *Eikon Basilike* and the English Revolution," in Nicholas Tyacke, ed., *The English Revolution, c. 1590–1720: Politics, Religion and Communities* (Manchester: Manchester UP, 2007),150–69. For the full text and a useful editorial introduction, see *Eikon Basilike with Selections from Eikonklastes*, ed. Holly Faith Nelson and Jim Daems (Peterborough, ON: Broadview, 2006).

hast suffered so far to prevail upon me, as to be able to pervert and abuse my acts of greatest indulgence to them, and assurance of them.

But no favours from me can make others more guilty than myself may be, of misusing those many and great ones, which thou, O Lord, hast conferred on me. I beseech thee give me and them such repentance as thou wilt accept, and such graces as we may not abuse. Make me so far happy as to make a right use of others' abuses, and by their failings of me, to reflect with a reforming displeasure upon my offences against thee. So, although for my sins I am by other men's sins deprived of thy temporal blessings, yet I may be happy to enjoy the comfort of thy mercies, which often raise the greatest sufferers to be the most glorious saints.

… Nor do I think my kingdoms so considerable as to preserve them with the forfeiture of that freedom which cannot be denied me as a king; because it belongs to me as a man and a Christian, owning the dictates of none but God to be above me, as obliging me to consent. Better for me to die, enjoying this empire of my soul, which subjects me only to God, so far as by reason or religion he directs me, than live with the title of a king, if it should carry such a vassalage with it as not to suffer me to use my reason and conscience, in which I declare as a king, to like or dislike.

So far am I from thinking the majesty of the Crown of England to be bound by any coronation oath, in a blind and brutish formality, to consent to whatever its subjects in parliament shall require, as some men will needs infer. While denying me any power of a negative voice as king, they are not ashamed to seek to deprive me of the liberty of using my reason with a good conscience; which themselves and all the commons of England enjoy proportional to their influence on the public; who would take it very ill to be urged, not to deny, whatever myself, as king, or the House of Peers with me should not so much desire as enjoin them to pass. I think my oath fully discharged in that point, by my governing only by such laws, as my people with the House of Peers have chosen, and myself have consented to. I shall never think myself conscientiously tied to go as oft against my conscience, as I should consent to such new proposals, which my reason, in justice, honour, and religion bids me deny. Yet so tender I see some men are of their being subject to arbitrary government (that is, the law of another's will, to which themselves give no consent) that they care not with how much dishonour and absurdity they make their king the only man, that must be subject to the will of others, without having power left him, to use his own reason, either in person or by any representation.

… If nothing but my blood will satisfy my enemies or quench the flames of my kingdoms, or thy temporal justice, I am content, if it be thy will, that it be shed by mine own subjects' hands. But, O, let the blood of me, though their king, yet a sinner, be dashed with the blood of my innocent and peace-making Redeemer, for in that thy justice will find not only a temporary expiation, but an eternal plenary satisfaction; both for my sins, and the sins of my people; whom I beseech thee still own for thine. And when thy wrath is appeased by my death, O remember thy great mercies toward them, and forgive them, O my Father, for they know not what they do.

... I am guilty in this war of nothing but this, that I gave such advantages to some men by confirming their power, which they knew not to use with that modesty and gratitude which became their loyalty and my confidence. Had I yielded less, I had been opposed less; had I denied more, I had been more obeyed.

... That I must die as a man is certain; that I may die a king, by the hands of my own subjects, a violent, sudden, and barbarous death, in the strength of my years, in the midst of my kingdoms; my friends and loving subjects being helpless spectators; my enemies insolent revilers and triumphers over me; living, dying, and dead, is so probable in human reason, that God has taught me not to hope otherwise as to man's cruelty. However, I despair not of God's infinite mercy. I know my life is the object of the Devil's and wicked men's malice, but yet under God's sole custody and disposal: Whom I do not think to flatter for longer life by seeming prepared to die, but I humbly desire to depend upon him and to submit to his will both in life and death, in what order so ever he is pleased to lay them out to me. I confess it is not easy for me to contend with those many horrors of death, wherewith God suffers me to be tempted; which are equally horrid, either in the suddenness of a barbarous assassination; or in those greater formalities, whereby my enemies (being more solemnly cruel) will, it may be, seek to add (as those did who crucified Christ) the mockery of justice to the cruelty of malice. That I may be destroyed, as with greater pomp and artifice, so with less pity, it will be but a necessary policy to make my death appear as an act of justice, done by subjects upon their sovereign, who know that no law of God or man invests them with any power of judicature without me, much less against me: and who, being sworn and bound by all that is sacred before God and man, to endeavour my preservation, must pretend justice to cover their perjury.

... O My Saviour, who knows what it is to die with me, as a man, make me to know what it is to pass through death to life with thee my God.... Thou gives me leave as a man to pray, that this cup may pass from me; but thou hast taught me as a Christian by the example of Christ to add, not my will, but thine be done.

The King's reasons for declining the jurisdiction of the High Court of Justice:

Having already made my protestations, not only against the illegality of this pretended Court, but also, that no earthly power can justly call me (who am your king) in question as a delinquent, I would not any more open my mouth upon this occasion, more than to refer myself to what I have spoken, were I in this case alone concerned: but the duty I owe to God in the preservation of the true liberty of my people will not suffer me at this time to be silent. For how can any free-born subject of England call life or anything he possesses his own, if power without right daily makes new and abrogates the old fundamental laws of the land, which I now take to be the present case. Wherefore when I came hither, I expected that you would have endeavoured to have satisfied me concerning these grounds which hinder me to answer to your pretended impeachment. But since I see that nothing I can say will move you to it (though negatives are not so naturally proved as affirmatives) yet I will show you the reason why I am confident you cannot judge me, nor indeed the meanest man in England: for I will not (like you), without showing a reason, seek to impose a belief upon my subjects.

There is no proceeding just against any man but what is warranted either by God's laws or the municipal laws of the country where he lives. Now I am most confident this day's proceeding cannot be warranted by God's laws; for, on the contrary, the authority of obedience unto kings is clearly warranted and strictly commanded in both the Old and New Testament, which, if denied, I am ready instantly to prove.

And for the question now in hand, there it is said, that "where the word of a King is, there is power; and who may say unto him, what are you doing?" (Ecclesiastes 8:4). Then for the law of this land: I am no less confident that no learned lawyer will affirm that an impeachment can lie against the king, they all going in his name. And one of their maxims is that the king can do no wrong. Besides, the law upon which you ground your proceedings must either be old or new: if old, show it; if new, tell what authority warranted by the fundamental laws of the land has made it, and when. But how the House of Commons can erect a Court of Judicature, which was never one [a court] itself (as is well known to all lawyers) I leave to God and the world to judge. And it were full as strange that they should pretend to make laws without king or Lords' House, to any that have heard speak of the laws of England.

And admitting, but not granting, that the people of England's commission could grant your pretended power, I see nothing you can show for that. For certainly you never asked the question of the tenth man in the kingdom, and in this way you manifestly wrong even the poorest ploughman, if you demand not his free consent. Nor can you pretend any colour for your pretended commission without the consent at least of the major part of every man in England of whatsoever quality or condition, which I am sure you never went about to seek, so far are you from having it. Thus you see that I speak not for my own right alone, as I am your king, but also for the true liberty of all my subjects, which consists not in the power of government, but in living under such laws, such a government, as may give themselves the best assurance of their lives and property of their goods. Nor in this must or do I forget the privileges of both Houses of Parliament, which this day's proceedings do not only violate, but likewise occasion the greatest breach of their public faith that (I believe) ever was heard of, with which I am far from charging the two Houses. For all the pretended crimes laid against me bear date long before this treaty at Newport, in which I having concluded as much as in me lay, and hopefully expecting the Houses' agreement thereunto, I was suddenly surprised and hurried from thence as a prisoner. Upon which account I am against my will brought hither, where since I am come, I cannot but to my power defend the ancient laws and liberties of this kingdom, together with my own just right. Then for anything I can see, the higher House is totally excluded; and for the House of Commons, it is too well known that the major part of them are detained or deterred from sitting. So, as if I had no other, this were sufficient for me to protest against the lawfulness of your pretended Court. Besides all this, the peace of the kingdom is not the least in my thoughts; and what hope of settlement is there so long as power reigns without rule or law, changing the whole frame of that government under which this kingdom has flourished for many hundred years? (Nor will I say what will fall out in case this lawless, unjust proceeding against me do go on.) And believe it, the commons of England will not thank you for this change; for they will remember how happy they have been of late years under the reigns of Queen Elizabeth, the King my father, and myself, until the beginning of these unhappy troubles, and will have cause to doubt that they shall never be so happy under any new. And by this time it will be too sensibly evident that the arms I took up were only to defend the fundamental laws of this kingdom against those who have supposed my power has totally changed the ancient government.

Thus, having showed you briefly the reasons why I cannot submit to your pretended authority, without violating the trust which I have from God for the welfare and liberty of my people, I expect from you either clear reasons to convince my judgment, showing me that I am in an error (and then truly I will answer) or that you will withdraw your proceedings.

This I intended to speak in Westminster Hall, on Monday, January 22, but against reason was hindered to show my reasons.

Frontispiece to the *Eikon Basilike*

This image appeared in several variations in many editions of the *Eikon Basilike*. Richly emblematic and allegorical, it helped promote the image of Charles as Christ-like martyr. It depicts the king treading under foot his earthly crown while grasping a crown of thorns of the sort worn by Christ before his sacrificial crucifixion and fixing his eyes on a heavenly crown. These three crowns were respectively "splendidam & gravem" (splendid and heavy); "asperam & levam" (bitter and light); and "beatam & aeternam" (blessed and eternal). The text in front of him reads "In verbo tuo spes mea" (in your words I put my hope). The ray of light behind him is inscribed with the motto that from the darkness comes light. The ray in front of him asserts "Coeli specto," or "I look to heaven." In the storm-tossed scene behind Charles, we see scrolls with Latin text, which observe that "Nescit naufragium virtus" (virtue cannot be drowned); "Crescit sub pondere [virtus]" (virtue grows under oppression, or when weighted down); and "immota triumphans" (unmoved, triumphant). What else can be observed from this image? Why might it have proved so popular and so powerful for so many people? (Indeed, some women used it as a pattern for their embroidery.) Why might others have denounced it as idolatrous?

Image from a 1662 edition of the *Eikon Basilike*. Courtesy Special Collections, Killam Library, Dalhousie University.

DOCUMENT 7:

A Soldier's Doubts: Extracts from Francis White, *The copies of several letters contrary to the opinion of the present powers, presented to the Lord Gen. Fairfax, and Lieut. Gen. Cromwell* (London, 1649)

Royalists obviously opposed the king's execution, but so too did some of the very men who fought against Charles. An officer in the parliamentary army, White had argued against continued negotiations with the king, urging indeed that monarchy be abolished; but he counselled against capital punishment. These extracts come from a work in which he published some of the letters he had written to the army leadership to explain his reservations.

e

To the Reader: Having for some years been an actor in the affairs of the late wars, and likewise an observer of the proceedings of state, in which I have been concerned more than every private person, I have therefore offered my judgement and declared my opinion in matters of highest concernment to my Lord General [Fairfax] and Lieutenant General Cromwell, and had no great desire to have published what I have written. But hearing by many of my friends that it is generally reported by most that have heard of me, that I have now declined my principles and am turned **Cavalier** [...] because I declared my dissent to the taking away the life of the king. But to manifest to the world the truth and innocence of my heart, I have published these following letters, to show that I was of the same judgement formerly as I now continue, as may appear in my letter sent to Lieut. Gen. Cromwell, almost a year ago, and what I have written to my Lord General, although contrary to the opinion of the present powers, I thought myself bound in conscience to perform, to preserve my own inward peace. For although some men make no conscience of their engagements, vows, and oaths, yet I hope God will give me power rather to suffer death, than destroy my life. I know that my judgement is not infallible, yet notwithstanding I must keep close to my principles, until I am convinced of error. I have here declared my principles and purpose, to stand in the prosecution of the public service with faithfulness, while God by his grace enables me.
Francis White.
20 March 1649.

Cavalier: From the root word used for knights and horsemen in other European languages, in English "Cavalier" suggested a swashbuckling, swaggering variant adorned by long ringlets of hair and other fashionable frivolities. Royalists soon reclaimed the term for themselves, in turn deriding their parliamentary opponents as "Roundheads," for their supposed preference for short hair and puritanical plainness.

The Copy of a Letter presented to his Excellency, the Lord Fairfax, General:

My Lord,
I am a member of your army, and included in all actions done by the disciplinary power. While I silently consent thereto, and I would never appear a dissenter to anything that tends to public good, although never so prejudicial to my

particular interest; but rather than I would submit to anything of essential public prejudice to the people or to destroy my inward peace, I would expose myself to temporal destruction. For God is my witness, I do not so much fear them that can kill the body only as I do him that is able to cast both body and soul into hell. So far as I have been employed in the common work, I have cheerfully acted or borne my public testimonies, and I hope forever shall. My Lord, I have taken notice of many petitions from almost all the forces in England, and from divers people of the counties, which supplicate for many good things, which they desire your Excellency to procure. In all which good things, I do heartily concur with their petitions; but I have observed this as one thing generally desired, that they may have execution of justice upon the king, and as far as I can perceive, it is generally intended by the officers of the army, and the members of the present House of Commons, to take away the life of the king. But with submission to your Excellency, I desire leave to declare my dissent, and upon grounds conscientious for these reasons following.

First, because there are no clear grounds by any legal authority to take away the life of the king.

engagement: In 1643, for example, the English parliamentarians and Scottish Covenanters entered into a "Solemn League and Covenant" to join forces against the Royalists and which included, amongst other things, a commitment "to preserve and defend the King's Majesty's person and authority." While all men 18 or older were expected to sign on to the Covenant, those holding office or command in the parliamentary faction were required to do so.

Secondly, it is contrary to our first **engagement** and our general professions, vows, and covenants, to God and the world.

Thirdly, I do not discern it will produce any general good to the nation, but rather the contrary. Having declared my opinion and the chief reasons for the same, I desire your Lordship to read these following lines, for the clearing of those reasons and the justifying my integrity and innocence in former actions.

At the first taking up of arms, I was sensible of the oppression and injustice which was exercised by the king and his ministers upon the people, he exalting himself to act beyond all laws, which his predecessors and himself had bound themselves by consent to observe. He raising arms to enforce the exercise of his power, to the maintaining an absolute tyranny over the nation, was the chief ground of my opposing him: and I have freely acted in the affairs of war to the subduing of his power and the vindicating of the people's just rights, and claim to the disposal of the military power without his consent. In the prosecution of this service, I have been as free from seeking revenge upon the person of the king, as to violate my own life. The chief end I seek is the preservation of the righteous people, with the safety and well-being of the whole, and if possible without taking away the life of Charles Stuart, king of England.

First I say, I do not understand how it may be done by any legal authority according to the kingly government: though it may be a just thing, yet I know not how it may justly be done. I never heard of any throne erected in the earth, either by God or men, for the judging of a king, until the erecting of this late tribunal at Westminster. All the judgement seats that are legally erected in this nation were made by King, Lords, and Commons; but the king ever did exempt himself from personal judgement, by virtue of the military, regal, and legislative power which he retained in himself, which was gotten by the sword of his predecessors, and kept by traditional descent. Although the people since the Conquest have had the liberty of choosing laws, so that he did not set up laws and judicatures legally at his will, yet there was no law made nor judicatures erected, but by his will. Although he agreed that the people should have the power of choosing laws, yet he determined that he would keep the power of confirming laws; so that no law was ever made without his will.

And if it be thoroughly examined we may find that the king has no other right to the military, regal, and legislative power than the sword did constitute and invest him with by divine permission, the people submitting thereto for fear, and to avoid greatest mischief. But now the king and his party being conquered by the sword, I believe the sword may justly remove the power from him, and settle it in its original fountain next under God, the people. But to judge or execute his person, I do not understand that any legal authority in being can justly do it. I doubt not but the sword may do it, but how righteous judgement that may be, that God and future generations will judge. It is clear that the military power is exalted above the regal and legislative power, and is now come to the throne of God, and under no other legal judgement, until there be a legal authority erected, as is offered in the **Agreement**, to which it may submit. And seeing God has in righteousness for the sins of the people and their king brought us into this unhappy condition, I therefore plead with your Excellency, to use the sword with as much tenderness as may be, to preserve the lives of men, and especially the life of the king.

And for my second reason, because we have made general profession of preserving his person, and whenever anyone accused us of seeking the life of the king, we always denied it, until this late **Remonstrance**. Now Sir, it is as real a manifestation of a Christian, a honourable and noble spirit, as can be discovered to the world, to be true to what it doth profess, and to be the same in adversity as in prosperity, and in prosperity as it was in adversity; and it is more honourable to save the life of a conquered enemy than to destroy him. For if he has prosecuted his designs according to his judgement and conscience, and were in the wrong way, it was because God suffered the Devil to blind his understanding, that he did not know the truth, and it is better to let him live and learn to repent than to make haste to send him to destruction; so that his remaining alive be not any general prejudice, or more mischievous than his death would be, which would well be considered under the third reason.

I do not understand any essential good that can accrue to the people by the taking away his life. For it is not so much the person that can hurt us as the power that is made up in the kingly office by this corrupt constitution. For if the person be taken away presently, another lays claim to the kingly office, and for any thing I know, has as much right to the dominion as his predecessor had, and will, without question, have all the assistance that this person can procure

Agreement of the People: A manifesto prepared by Agitators (i.e., representatives of rank-and-file soldiers in the New Model Army) and civilian Levellers, setting out the fundamentals of a proposed constitution for the postwar government; first issued in October 1647 and then in amended versions thereafter.

Remonstrance: The New Model Army's manifesto of November 1648, explaining its desire to abandon negotiations with King Charles and to move to a trial.

for the attaining thereof, and will be able to do more mischief because he is at liberty, and this under your power.

Again, this king being the king of Scotland and Ireland, according to the laws in being, they have an interest in his person as well as England, notwithstanding he is under our power. Now if you will judge the kingdoms of Scotland and Ireland in that which concerns their interest, where you can claim no right, it is an evident wrong and may give them just offence and ground of quarrel against this nation, and by this, may be of more prejudice to the whole than can be good to the particular.

I desire, my Lord, that we may issue a Christian spirit, not rendering evil for evil, but rather good for evil. Although wicked men will deal wickedly with us, yet let us deal mercifully with them, and pardon and forgive as we desire God should pardon and forgive us. In this way I do verily believe we shall be greater conquerors than yet we have been, if we can conquer ourselves, and the affection of our enemies which this does lead unto. My Lord, in all that I have written, I am not against the judging of the king; but I say it is by no legal authority, but only what the sword exalts: although it be not an exact Marshal Court, yet it is little different, and not a legitimate authority to the king, yet it may as justly judge him, as ever he judged the people, and may dethrone him and divest him of all power and authority in the English nation. And I think it is necessary so far to proceed, and to detain him as a prisoner at war, till he may be delivered with safety to yourselves and the nation.

I desire your Excellency's favourable construction of what I have written, and if it be not your Excellency's judgement, all that I desire for my satisfaction is that your Excellency will appoint such a general council as the army in these parts shall be included by the major voice thereof. If it be not concluded according to my judgement, yet therein shall I have my desire, because I consent to be included by the major part, to avoid division. If this may not be granted, then must I declare my dissent, and that it is an action done by virtue of the disciplinary power of the army, by which I am not in this case willingly included, and so I hope I shall preserve myself in innocence and peace, and not be an instrument of the mischiefs and evils that may be brought upon this nation by the taking away the blood of their king. Having taken this freedom to write to your Excellency, I shall now take my leave, and remain,

Your Lordship's most humble servant, Francis White.
22 January 1649.

DOCUMENT 8:

Principles and Pragmatism: Extracts from John Lilburne, *The legal fundamental liberties of the people of England revived, asserted, and vindicated* (London, 1649)

Also known as "Freeborn John," John Lilburne was a larger than life character who became famous for his many legal battles in which he argued for the individual's "freeborn rights"—rights, he said, that we had by birth and not by gift. Punished with a brutal flogging for unlicensed printing before the civil wars began, Lilburne later fought against the royalists with some distinction but also found himself imprisoned for criticizing members of parliament. He later faced charges of treason against the new republican regime—charges against which he, remarkably, successfully defended himself. A prominent Leveller, he worked to secure a written constitution for the country, a free press, and religious toleration. A proudly self-proclaimed "**Agitator**," he opposed the execution of the king and warned that tyranny came in many guises. The following extract gives a taste of his arguments.[1]

Agitator: Name given to regimental representatives elected by soldiers in the New Model Army to act as their agents in dealings with the Army's leaders.

The full title of this work conveys Lilburne's concerns: *The Legal Fundamental Liberties of the People of England Revived, Asserted, and Vindicated. OR, An Epistle written the eighth day of June 1649, by Lieut. Colonel John Lilburn (Arbitrary and Aristocratical prisoner in the Tower of London) to Mr. William Lenthall, Speaker to the remainder of those few Knights, Citizens, and Burgesses that Col. Thomas Pride at his late purge thought convenient to leave sitting at Westminster, as most fit for his and his Masters' designs, to serve their ambitious and tyrannical ends, to destroy the good old Laws, Liberties and Customs of England, the badges of our freedom (as the Declaration against the King, of the 7 of March 1648, pg. 23 calls them), and by force of arms to rob the people of their lives, estates and properties, and subject them to perfect vassalage and slavery, as he clearly evinces in his present Case &c. they have done, who (and in truth no otherwise) pretendedly style themselves the Conservators of the peace of England, or the Parliament of England, intrusted and authorised by the consent of all the people thereof, whose Representatives by election … they say they are; although they are never able to produce one bit of a law, or any piece of a commission to prove, that all the people of England, or one quarter, tenth, hundred, or thousand part of them authorised Thomas Pride, with his regiment of soldiers, to choose them a Parliament, as indeed he hath de facto done by this pretended mock-Parliament: And therefore it cannot properly be called the Nation's or People's Parliament, but Col. Pride's and his associates, whose really it is; who, although they have beheaded the King for a Tyrant, yet walk in his oppressing steps, if not worse and higher.*

---

1   For more on Lilburne and the Levellers, see Paulina Gregg, *Freeborn John: The Biography of John Lilburne* (London: Phoenix Press, 2000; first edn. 1961); Rachel Foxley, *The Levellers: Radical Political Thought in the English Revolution* (Manchester: Manchester UP, 2013); Edward Vallance, "Reborn John? The Eighteenth Century Afterlife of John Lilburne," *History Workshop Journal* 74 (2012), 1–26, and Andrew Sharp, "The Levellers and the End of Charles I," in *The Regicides and the Execution of Charles I*, 181–201.

A nd having been in the North about my own business, where I saw [Oliver] Cromwell, and made as diligent scrutiny into things about him as I could; which I then to myself judged savoured more of intended self-exalting than anything really and heartily (of what before I had strongly heard of him) to the thorough advancement of those things that were worthy to be accounted indeed the liberties and freedoms of the nation.

And being come to London, myself and some other of my friends ... sent a message down to him to Pomfret [Pontefract Castle], to be delivered to himself, and to debate it with him, and bring his express answer back again speedily. The effect of which message was: That to our knowledge, God had caused him to understand the principles of a just government, under which the glory of God may shine forth by an equal distribution unto all men. That the obtaining of this was the sole intended end of the war: and that the war cannot be justified upon any other account than the defence of the people's right to that just government and their freedom under it.

His answer to which message by Mr. Hunt was principally directed to the Independents, some of whom appointed a meeting at the Nags-head Tavern by Blackwell-Hall ... where we had a large debate of things, and where the just ends of the war were as exactly laid open by Mr. [John] Wildman, as ever I heard in my life. But towards the conclusion, they plainly told us, the chief thing first to be done by the army, was first to cut off the king's head, etc., and force and thoroughly purge, if not dissolve, the parliament. All of which we were all against ... and I plainly told them in these words, or to this effect:

It's true, I look upon the king as an evil man in his actions, and divers of his party as bad: but the army had cozened us the last year and fallen from all their promises and declarations, and therefore could not rationally any more be trusted by us without good cautions and security. In which regard, although we should judge the king as arrant a tyrant as they supposed him or could imagine him to be, and the parliament as bad as they could make them, yet there being no other balancing power in the kingdom against the army but the king and parliament, it was our interest to keep up one tyrant to balance another, until we certainly knew what that tyrant that pretended fairest would give us as our freedoms; that so we might have something to rest upon, and not suffer the army (so much as in us lay) to devolve all the government of the kingdom into their will and swords, which were two things we nor no rational man could like, and leave no persons nor power to be a counter balance against them. And if we should do this, our slavery for future (I told them) might probably be greater than ever it was in the king's time, and so our last error would be greater than our first. Therefore I pressed very hard for an Agreement of the People first, for a new parliament, etc., utterly disclaiming the thoughts of the other until this was done. And this (I told them) was not only my opinion, but I believe it to be the unanimous opinion of all my friends with whom I most constantly conversed.

… But again to return: After I had done as much in the North as I could at present do about my own business, I came again to London, where I fixed up my resolution wholly to devote my self to provide for the future well-being of my wife and children, and not without the most extraordinary necessity engage in any public contests again, making it my work to enquire into the true state of things with the great men that sat at the helm and whether the bent of their spirits now after they had taken off the king, was to set the nation free from tyranny, as well as from some they called principal tyrants; and whether or not the drift of all their actions were but a mere changing of persons, but not of things or tyranny itself. And truly my observations and inquiries brought me so little satisfaction in the visible intention of the ruling men, for all their many solemn engagements to the contrary, that I looked clearly at the whole tendency of their ways, to drive at a greater tyranny than ever, in the worst of the king's reign (before the parliament) was exercised. At which I bit my lip, but said little, and went to no meeting; which made many of my old faithful friends be jealous of me, some of whom gave out some private hints that I had now served myself by my pretended reparations, and I was thereby quieted, and was become like all the rest of the world, and so there was an end of me.

But I confess, I was in a kind of deep muse with myself, what to do with myself; being like an old weather-beaten ship, that would fain be in some harbour of ease and rest, and my thoughts were very much bent of going into Holland, where I conjectured I should be out of harm's way and get a little repose. And while I was thus musing, I heard from thence of a most transcendent rage that the king's party there were in, especially about the beheading the late king; so that I judged there was no safety for me there, especially when I called to mind what the post-master of Burton and others in Yorkshire told me as I came up from Newcastle, which was that the Cavaliers in those parts were most desperate mad at me in particular about the beheading of the late king: although I were as far as Newcastle when it was done, and refused to give my consent to be one of his judges, although I was solicited so to be before I went out of London; yea, although I avowedly declared myself at Windsor against the manner and time of their intended dealing with him, arguing there very stiffly, that upon their own principles, which led them to look upon all legal authority in England as now broken, they could be no better than murderers in taking away the king's life though never so guilty of the crimes they charged upon him. For as justice ought to be done, especially for blood, which they then principally charged upon him, so said I, and still say, it ought to be done justly. For in case another man murder me, and a day, a week, or a year after my brother or friend that is no legal magistrate executes him, therefore, yet this is murder in the eye of the law, because it was done by a hand that had no authority to do it. And therefore I pressed again and again, seeing that they themselves confessed that all legal authority in England was broken, that they would stay his trial until a new and equal free representative, upon the agreement of the well-affected people that had not fought against their liberties, rights and freedoms, could be chosen and sit, and then either try him thereby, or else by their judges sitting in the court called King's Bench. But they at Windsor asked me how by law I could have him tried: I told them, the law of England expressly says, Whosoever orders or kills another shall die; it does not say, excepting the king, queen, or prince, etc., but indefinitely, whosoever murders shall die. And therefore where none is excepted, there all men are included in law. But the king is a man: ergo, he is included as well as I. Unto which it was objected, that it would hardly be proved, that the king with his own hands killed a man. To which I answered, by the law of England, he that counsels or commissions others to kill a man or men is as guilty of the fact as he or they that do it. And besides, the advantage of trying the king by the rules of the law would be sufficient to declare, that no man is born (or justly can be made) lawless, but that even magistrates as well as people are subject to the penal part of the law as well as the directive part.

And besides, to try him in an extraordinary way, that has no real footsteps nor paths in our law, would be a thing of extraordinary ill precedent; for why not twenty upon pretended extraordinary cases, as well as one? And why not a thousand as well as twenty? And extraordinary cases are easily made and pretended by those that are uppermost, though never so unjust in themselves. And besides, to try him in an extraordinary way, when the law has provided all the essentials of justice in an ordinary way (and merely wants nothing—if it do want anything—but twelve kings as his peers or equals) will nourish and increase in men that erroneous counsel, that magistrates by the laws of God, nature, and reason, are not no nor ought not to be subject to the penal part of the laws of men, as well as the directive part of it, which is the bane, ruin, and destruction of all the commonwealths in the world.

DOCUMENT 9:

Overthrowing "Kingly Power" as well as Kings: Extracts from Gerrard Winstanley, *A New Year's Gift for the Parliament and Army, Showing what the Kingly Power is, and that the cause of those they call Diggers is the life and marrow of that cause the Parliament has Declared for, and the Army Fought for* (London, 1650)

Winstanley was the spokesperson for a group of people known as Diggers, or True Levellers, who insisted that God had made the Earth to be "a common treasury" for all. In the months after Charles's execution, they began communally farming waste land. Hostile neighbours secured their eviction, but for a few years Winstanley continued to spread their radical message through print. His writings show that while some thought the execution of the king too far a step, others thought it only the beginning.[1] What, for him, was the "kingly power" that needed to be destroyed along with Charles and the monarchy?

◈

Gentlemen of the parliament and army: you and the common people have assisted each other to cast out the head of oppression which was kingly power, seated in one man's hand, and that work is now done, and until that work was done you called upon the people to assist you to deliver this distressed, bleeding dying nation out of bondage. And the people came and failed you not, counting neither purse nor blood too dear to part with to effect this work.

The parliament after this have made an Act to cast out kingly power, and to make England a free commonwealth. These Acts the people are much rejoiced with, as being words forerunning their freedom, and they wait for their accomplishment that their joy may be full. For as words without action are a cheat, and kill the comfort of a righteous spirit, so words performed in action do comfort and nourish the life thereof.

Now, Sirs, wheresoever we spy out kingly power, no man I hope shall be troubled to declare it, nor afraid to cast it out, having both Act of Parliament, the soldiers' oath, and the common people's consent on his side. For kingly power is like a great spread tree: if you lop the head or top-bough, and let the other branches and root stand, it will grow again and recover fresher strength.

If any ask me what kingly power is, I answer, there is a twofold kingly power. The one is, the kingly power of righteousness, and this is the power of Almighty God, ruling the whole creation in peace and keeping it together. And this is the power of universal love, leading people into all truth, teaching everyone to do as he would be done unto. Now once more striving with flesh

---

1 For more on Winstanley and the Diggers, see the introduction to *The Complete Works of Gerrard Winstanley*, ed. Thomas N. Corns, Ann Hughes, and David Loewenstein (Oxford: Oxford UP, 2009).

and blood, shaking down everything that cannot stand, and bringing every one into the unity of himself, the one Spirit of love and righteousness, and so will work a thorough restoration. But this kingly power is above all, and will tread all covetousness, pride, envy, and self-love, and all other enemies whatsoever under his feet and take the kingdom and government of the creation out of the hand of self-seeking and self-honouring flesh, and rule the alone King of Righteousness in the earth: and this indeed is Christ himself, who will cast out the curse. But this is not that kingly power intended by that Act of Parliament to be cast out, but pretended to be set up, though this kingly power be much fought against both by parliament, army, clergy, and people; but when they are made to see him, then they shall mourn, because they have persecuted him.

But the other kingly power is the power of unrighteousness, which indeed is the Devil. And, O, that there were such a heart in parliament and army, as to perform your own Act; then people would never complain of you for breach of covenant, for your covetousness, pride, and too much self-seeking that is in you. And you on the other side would never have cause to complain of the people's murmurings against you. Truly this jarring that is between you and the people is the kingly power; yea, that very kingly power which you have made an Act to cast out....

The life of this dark kingly power, which you have made an Act of Parliament and oath to cast out, if you search it to the bottom, you shall see it lies within the iron chest of cursed covetousness, who gives the Earth to some part of mankind, and denies it to another part of mankind. And that part that has the Earth has no right from the law of creation to take it to himself and shut out others; but he took it away violently by theft and murder in conquest: As when our Norman William came into England and conquered, he turned the English out and gave the land unto his Norman soldiers every man his parcel to enclose, and hence rose up **propriety** [property]. For this is the fruit of war from the beginning, for it removes propriety out of a weaker into a stronger hand, but still upholds the curse of bondage. And hereby the kingly power which you have made an Act and sworn to cast out, does remove himself from one chair to another; and so long as the sword rules over brethren, (mind what I say) so long the kingly power of darkness rules, and so large as yet is his kingdom, which spreads from sea to sea and fills the Earth. But Christ is rising who will take the dominion and kingdom out of his hand, and his power of righteousness shall rise and spread from east to west, from north to south, and fill the Earth with himself, and cast the other cursed power out, when Covetousness sheaths his sword and ceases to rage in the field; he first makes sharp laws of bondage, that those that are conquered and that by him are appointed not to enjoy the Earth, but are turned out, shall be servants, slaves, and vassals to the Conqueror's party: so those laws that uphold whips, prisons, [and] gallows is but the same power of the sword that raged and that was drunk with blood in the field.

propriety: While "propriety" today tends to imply "the quality of being proper," in earlier usage, it also meant "property," or ownership.

King Charles, it is true, was the head of this kingly power in England, and he reigned as he was a successor of the last Norman conqueror: and whosoever you be, that have propriety of land have your titles and evidences made to you in his or his ancestors' name, and from his and their will and kingly power. I am sure he was not our creator, and therefore parcelled out the Earth to some, and denied it to others, therefore he must needs stand as a conqueror, and was the head of this kingly power, that burdens and oppresses the people, and that is the cause of all our wars and divisions. For if this kingly power of covetousness, which is the unrighteous divider, did not yet [still] rule, both parliament, army, and rich people would cheerfully give consent that those we call poor should dig and freely plant the waste and common land for a livelihood, seeing there is land enough, and more by half than is made use of, and not be suffered to perish for want. And yet, O ye rulers of England, you make a blazing profession, that you know and that you own God, Christ, and the Scriptures: but did Christ ever declare such hardness of heart? Did not he bid the rich man go and sell all that he had and give to the poor? And does not the Scripture say, if you make a covenant, keep it, though it be to your loss? But truly it will not be to your loss to let your fellow creatures, your equals in the Creation, nay those that have been faithful in your cause, and so your friends; I say it will not be to your loss to let them quietly improve the waste and common land, that they may live in peace, freed from the heavy burdens of poverty. For hereby our own land will be increased with all sorts of commodities, and the people will be knit together in love, to keep out a foreign enemy that endeavours, and that will endeavour as yet, to come like an army of cursed rats and mice to destroy our inheritance. So that if this freedom be quietly granted to us, you grant it but to yourselves, to Englishmen, to your own flesh and blood: and you do but give us our own, which covetousness, in the kingly power has, and yet does hold from us; for the Earth in the first creation of it, was freely given to whole mankind, without respect of persons. Therefore, you lords of manors and you rulers of England, if you own God, Christ, and Scripture, now make restitution and deliver us quiet possession of our land, which the kingly power as yet holds from us.

While this kingly power reigned in one man called Charles, all sort of people complained of oppression, both gentry and common people, because their lands, **enclosures**, and **copyholds** were entangled, and because their trades were destroyed by monopolizing **patentees**, and your troubles were that you could not live free from oppression in the earth. Thereupon you that were the gentry, when you were assembled in parliament, you called upon the poor common people to come and help you and cast out oppression. And you that complained are helped and freed, and that top-bough is lopped off the tree of tyranny, and kingly power in that one particular is cast out. But, alas, oppression is a great tree still, and keeps off the son of freedom from the poor commons still.

enclosure: Typically, the fencing in for individual use of land once open to communal use.

copyhold: A form of land tenure, or the terms by which a tenant held land from a landlord.

patentee: Patents from the Crown sometimes allowed an individual to monopolize the production or sale of a particular commodity (e.g., soap, sweet wine), and thus to exact fees from anyone else who wanted to produce or sell that good.

tithing: Tithes were compulsory payments to the Church, equivalent to the tenth of one's income.

Norman Conquest: Conquest of England in 1066 led by Duke William of Normandy, *aka* William the Conqueror.

… Now there are three branches more of kingly power greater than the former that oppresses this land wonderfully; and these are the power of the **tithing** priests over the tenths of our labours; and the power of lords of manors, holding the free use of the commons and waste land from the poor; and the intolerable oppression either of bad laws or of bad judges corrupting good laws. These are branches of the **Norman Conquest** and kingly power still, and want a reformation.

… [L]ords of manors, they were William the Conqueror's colonels and favourites, and he gave a large circuit of land to everyone, called a lordship, that they might have a watchful eye, that if any of the conquered English should begin to plant themselves upon any common or waste land, to live out of sight or out of slavery, that then some lord of a manor or other might see and know of it, and drive them off, as these lords of manors nowadays endeavour to drive off the Diggers from digging upon the commons. But we expect the rulers of the land will grant unto us, their friends, the benefit of their own Acts against kingly power, and not suffer that Norman power to crush the poor oppressed who helped them in their straits, nor suffer that Norman power to bud fresher out, and so in time may come to overtop our dearly bought freedom more than ever.

Search all your laws, and I'll adventure my life, for I have little else to lose, that all lords of manors hold title to the commons by no stronger hold than the king's will, whose head is cut off, and the king held title as he was a conqueror. Now if you cast off the king who was the head of that power, surely the power of lords of manors is the same. Therefore, perform your own Act of Parliament, and cast out that part of the kingly power likewise, that the people may see you understand what you say and do, and that you are faithful.

For truly the kingly power reigns strongly in the lords of manors over the poor. For my own particular, I have in other writings as well as in this declared my reasons, that the common land is the poor people's propriety; and I have dug upon the commons, and I hope in time to obtain the freedom to get food and raiment therefrom by righteous labour, which is all I desire….

… We claim an equal portion in the victory over the king, by virtue of the two Acts of Parliament, the one to make England a free commonwealth, the other to take away kingly power. Now the kingly power (you have heard) is a power that rules by the sword in covetousness and self, giving the earth to some and denying it to others. And this kingly power was not in the hand of the king alone, but lords, and lords of manors, and corrupt judges, and lawyers especially, held it up likewise; for he was the head, and they, with the tithing-priests, are the branches of that tyrannical kingly power. And all the several limbs and members must be cast out before kingly power can be pulled up root and branch. Mistake me not, I do not say, Cast out the persons of men. No, I do not desire their fingers to ache: but I say, Cast out their power, whereby they hold the people in bondage, as the king held them in bondage. And I say, it is our own freedom we claim, both by bargain and by equality in the conquest, as well as by the law of righteous creation, which gives the Earth to all equally.

PART 3
Trying the King-Killers

DOCUMENT 10:

A Contemporary Depiction of the Executions of the King and of His Judges

With the restoration of monarchy in 1660 and Charles II's assumption of the thrones of Britain, loyalists and those who wanted to appear as such quickly produced denunciations of the "murderers" of the late king. While this section focuses on an account of the trial of one of those judges, the frontispiece of another related work is reprinted here for its representation of the contrasting executions of first the king and then his judges. What impressions did the artist who produced this image hope to convey about the two events, and with what techniques?

© The British Library Board; frontispiece from a publication on the trial of the regicides, Anon., *The True Characters of the Educations, Inclinations and Several Dispositions of all and every one of those Bloody and Barbarous Persons who sate as Judges upon the Life of our late Dread Soveraign King Charles I of ever Blessed Memory* (London, 1661). General Reference Collection E. 1080 (15).

The Trial of Major General Harrison: Extracts from Heneage Finch, *An Exact and most Impartial Accompt of the Indictment, Arraignment, Trial, and Judgment (according to Law) of Twenty Nine Regicides, The Murderers Of His Late Sacred Majesty Of Most Glorious Memory: Begun at Hicks-Hall on Tuesday, the 9th. of October, 1660 and Continued (at the Sessions-House in the Old-Bayley) until Friday, the nineteenth of the same Month* (London, 1660)

AN

EXACT and most *IMPARTIAL*

ACCOMPT

Of the *Indictment*, *Arraignment*, *Trial*, and *Judgment* (according to *Law*) of

Twenty nine

REGICIDES,

THE

MURTHERERS

Of His Late

SACRED MAJESTY

Of Most Glorious Memory:

Begun at *Hicks-Hall* on *Tuesday*, the 9th. of *October*, 1660. And Continued (at the *Sessions-House* in the *Old-Bayley*) untill *Friday*, the nineteenth of the same Moneth.

Together with a SUMMARY of the Dark, and Horrid *Decrees* of those *Caballists*, Preparatory to that Hellish Fact.

Exposed to view for the *Reader's* Satisfaction, and Information of *Posterity*.

Imprimatur, *John Berkenhead*.

London, Printed for *Andrew Crook* at the *Green Dragon* in St. *Paul's*-Church-yard, and *Edward Powel* at the *White-Swan* in *Little-Britain*. 1660.

Title page of Heneage Finch, *An Exact and Most Impartial Accompt of the Indictment, Arraignment, Trial and Judgement (according to Law) of Twenty Nine Regicides*, as published in 1660. Courtesy, Special Collections, Killam Library, Dalhousie University.

Despite the title, this work is neither "exact" nor "impartial": Heneage Finch
was the solicitor general who helped prosecute these trials. He and Sir Orlando
Bridgeman, one of the judges, rushed this into print immediately at the trials' end to
counter competing publications and accounts more sympathetic to the individuals
being tried. Only the first part of the work is included here, that detailing the trial
of Major-General Thomas Harrison. After the Restoration in 1660, an Act of Free
and General Pardon, Oblivion and Indemnity was passed in an effort "to bury all
seeds of future discords and remembrance of the former," offering amnesty to most
people but specifically excluding those men most responsible for the late king's
execution (or "murder").[1] One of those specifically excluded, Harrison was one of 29
men arraigned and his was one of ten executions packed into October of 1660. This
account of his trial provides further detail to elucidate the nature of Charles's trial,
partly through Harrison's testimony and partly by allowing a comparison of the
procedures and conventions of the trials themselves. Think, too, of how this account
of a trial differs from that published about the king's. When reading it, keep in
mind its authorship and purpose, and consider how it might have been read by
members of a diverse audience at the time of its first publication.

℘

9 October 1660.
After Proclamation for silence was made, it pleased Sir Orlando Bridgeman,
Lord Chief Baron of His Majesty's High Court of Exchequer, to speak to the
jury as follows.

The Lord Chief Baron's speech:

Gentlemen,

You are the grand inquest for the body of this county of Middlesex. You may
perceive by this commission that has been read, that we are authorized by the
king's majesty to hear and determine all treasons, felonies, and other offences
within this county. But because this commission is upon a special occasion, the
execrable murder of the blessed king that is now a saint in heaven, King Charles I,
we shall not trouble you with the heads of a long charge. The ground of this
commission was, and is, from the Act of Oblivion and Indemnity. You shall
find in that Act there is an exception of several persons, who (for their execrable
treasons in sentencing to death and signing the warrant for the taking away the
life of our said sovereign) are left to be proceeded against as traitors, according
to the laws of England, and are out of that Act wholly excepted and foreprized.

---

1   12 Chas. II, c. 11 (Charles II, 1660), "An Act of Free and Generall Pardon, Indempnity, and
    Oblivion," in *Statutes of the Realm*, Vol. 5, 1628–80, ed. John Raithby (1819), 226–34.

25 Edward III: This is the way statutes, or Acts of parliament, are cited, with the name of the king or queen in whose reign it was passed, preceded by the year of that reign, usually followed by a "c" or chapter number. In this case, the judge is referring to a famous statute against treason passed in 1352, i.e., in the 25th year of the reign of King Edward III. [Note that statutes from Charles II's reign are dated as if his reign began immediately after his father's death in 1649, acknowledging no interregnum; thus, the Act of Indemnity, passed in 1660, is cited as being passed in 12 Chas. II.]

Gentlemen, you see these persons are to be proceeded with according to the laws of the land; and I shall speak nothing to you but what are the words of the laws. By the statute **25 Edward III**, a statute or declaration of treason, it is made high treason to compass and imagine the death of the king. It was the ancient laws of the nation. In no case else imagination, or compassing, without an actual effect of it, was punishable by our law. *Nihil officit conatus, nisi sequatur effectus* [the attempt does not matter, if no effect follows from it]; that was the old rule of law. But in the case of the king, his life was so precious that the intent was treason by the common law, and declared treason by this statute. The reason of it is this, in the case of the death of the king, the head of the commonwealth is cut off, and what a trunk, an inanimate lump, the body is when the head is gone, you all know. For the life of a single man, there's the life of the offender; there's some recompense, life for life. But for the death of the king, what recompense can be made?

This compassing and imagining the cutting off the head of the king is known by some overt act. Treason it is in the wicked imagination, though not treason apparent; but when this poison swells out of the heart and breaks forth into action, in that case, it's high treason. Then what is an imagination or compassing of the king's death? Truly, it is anything which shows what the imagination is. Words in many cases are evidence of this imagination: they are evidence of the heart. Secondly, as words: so if a man, if two men do conspire to levy war against the king (and, by the way, what I say of the king is as well of the king dead, as living; for, if a treason be committed in the life of one king, it is a treason and punishable in the time of the successor) then, I say, in case, not only of words; but if they conspire to levy war against the king, there's another branch of this statute, the levying of war is treason. But if men shall go and consult together, and this is to kill the king, to put him to death: this consultation is clearly an overt act to prove this imagination or compassing of the king's death.

But what will you say then, if men do not only go about to conspire and consult, but take upon them to judge, condemn, nay, put to death the king? Certainly, this is so much beyond the imagination and compassing as 'tis not only laying the **cockatrice**'s egg but brooding upon it until it has brought forth a serpent. I must deliver to you for plain and true law that no authority, no single person, no community of persons, not the people collectively, or representatively, have any coercive power over the king of England. And I do not speak mine own sense, but the words of the laws unto you. [...]

Gentlemen, let me tell you what our law books say: for there's the ground out of which (and the statutes together) we must draw all our conclusions for matter of government. How do they style the king? They call him the lieutenant of God, and many other expressions. Says that book there: the king is immediate from God and has no superior. The statutes say that the Crown of England is immediately subject to God, and to no other power. The king (say our books),

cockatrice: The cockatrice was a mythological, deadly serpent said to be produced from an egg laid by a rooster.

he is not only *Caput Populi*, the head of the people, but *Caput Reipublicae*, the head of the commonwealth, the three estates. And, truly, thus our statutes speak very fully. Common experience tells you, when we speak of the king, and so the Statutes of Edward III, we call the king Our Sovereign Lord the King: sovereign, that is, supreme. And when the Lords and Commons in parliament apply themselves to the king, they use this expression, "Your Lords and Commons, your faithful subjects, humbly beseech." I do not speak any words of my own, but the words of the laws. Look upon the statute, 1 James I: there's a recognition that the Crown of England was lawfully descended on the king and his progeny. (The statute itself was read, to which it is desired, the reader will be referred.)

These are the words of the Act. And this is not the first precedent: for you shall find it [in] 1 Elizabeth c. 3; they do acknowledge the imperial crown lawfully descended on the queen, the same recognition with this. Before that (because we shall show you we go upon grounds of law in what we say), 24 Henry VIII c. 12: Whereas by sundry old authentic histories and chronicles it is manifestly declared and expressed that this realm of England is an empire, and so has been accepted in the world, governed by one supreme head and king, having the dignity and royal estate of the imperial crown, of the same, etc.

25 Henry VIII c. 21: There it is, the people, speaking of themselves, that they do recognize no superior under God, but only the king's grace.

Gentlemen, you see, if the king be immediate under God, he derives his authority from nobody else. If the king has an imperial power, if the king be head of the commonwealth, head of the body politic, if the body politic owe him obedience: truly, I think it is an undenied consequence, he must needs be superior over them.

Gentlemen, this is no new thing, to talk of an emperor or an imperial crown. Do not mistake me all this while: It is one thing to have an imperial crown, and another thing to govern absolutely.

Gentlemen, the imperial crown is a word that is significative: you shall find in all statutes [...] it is called an imperial crown. They that take the oaths of allegiance and supremacy, they swear that they will, to their power, assist, and defend all jurisdictions, privileges, pre-eminences, and authorities, granted or belonging to the king, his heirs, and successors, or annexed to the imperial crown of this realm. What is an imperial crown? It is that, which, as to the coercive part, is subject to no man under God. The king of Poland has a crown: but what is it? At his coronation it is conditioned with the people; that, if he shall not govern them according to such rules, they shall be freed from their homage and allegiance. But the crown of England is, and always was, an imperial crown, and so sworn. [...]

God forbid I should intend any absolute government by this. It is one thing to have an absolute monarchy, another thing to have that government absolutely without laws, as to any coercive power over the person of the king:

for as to things and actions, they will fall under another consideration as I will tell you by and by.

Gentlemen, since this is so, consider the oath of supremacy, which most men have taken, or should take. All men that enter into the parliament house, they are expressly enjoined by statute to take the oath of supremacy. What says that oath? We swear that the king is the only supreme governor within this realm and dominions. He is supreme, and the only supreme: and, truly, if he be supreme, there is neither major, nor superior. I urge this the more, lest any person, by any misconstruction or inference which they might make from something that has been acted by the higher powers, they might draw some dangerous inferences or consequences to colour or shadow over those murderous and traitorous acts which afterwards they committed. They had no authority. But as I told you, though I do set forth this and declare this to you, to let you know, that the king was immediately subject to God, and so was not punishable by any person; yet, let me tell you, there is that excellent temperament in our laws, that, for all this, the king cannot rule but by his laws. It preserves the king and his person, and the people's rights.

There are three things touching which the law is conversant: *Personae, Res,* and *Actiones*; Persons, Things, and Actions. For the person of the king: He is the supreme head. He is not punishable by any coercive power: the laws provide for that. The king can do no wrong, it is a rule of law, it is in our law-books very frequent: 22 Edward IV, **Lord Coke**, and many others. If he can do no wrong, he cannot be punished for any wrong. The king, he has the infirmities and weakness of a man: but he cannot do any injury, at least not considerable, in person. He must do it by ministers, agents, instruments. Now the law, though it provide for the king, yet if any of his ministers do wrong, though by his command, they are punishable. The king cannot arrest a man, as he cannot be arrested himself: but, if he arrest me by another man, I have remedy against this man, though not against the King: and so, he cannot take away my estate. This as to the person of the king: he is not to be touched: **"Touch not mine anointed."**

I come to Things. If the king claim a right, the king must sue according to his laws; the king is subject to the laws in that case. His possessions shall be tried by juries. If he will try a man for his father's death, you see he will try them by the laws. The law is the rule and square of his actions, and by which he himself is judged.

Then for Actions: that is, such actions whereby rights and titles are prosecuted or recovered, the king cannot judge in person betwixt man and man. He does it by his judges, and upon oath, and so in all cases whatsoever, if the King will have his right, it must be brought before his judges. Though this is an absolute monarchy, yet this is so far from infringing the people's rights that the people, as to their properties, liberties, and lives, have as great a privilege as the king. It is not the sharing of government that is for the liberty and benefit of the

Sir Edward Coke

(1552–1634): a chief justice and one of the foremost jurists and legal writers in English history.

Touch not mine anointed: Referencing a biblical verse, 1 Chronicles 16:22 or Psalms 105:15, both of which note that those set apart for God's service must not be harmed.

people: but it is how they may have their lives and liberties and estates safely secured under government. And you know, when the fatness of the olive was laid aside, and we were **governed by brambles**, these brambles, they did not only tear the skin but tore the flesh to the very bone.

governed by brambles: He is adapting a biblical fable, from Judges 9, about who should be king of the trees. The olive tree, fig tree, and grape vine refuse to be king, leaving only the least worthy, the bramble, to accept, to the danger of all the trees.

Gentlemen, I have done in this particular, to let you see, that the supreme power, being in the king, the king is immediately under God, owing his power to none but God. It is true (blessed be God) we have as great liberties as any people have in Christendom, in the world: but let us own them, where they are due. We have them by the concessions of our princes. Our princes have granted them: and the king, now, he in them has granted them likewise.

Gentlemen, I have been a little too long in this, and yet I cannot say, it is too long: because it may clear misunderstanding; so many poisonous opinions having gone abroad. To come a little nearer […] when we shall consider this horrid murder (truly, I cannot almost speak of it, but——*Vox faucibus haeret* [my voice sticks in my throat]). When we shall consider that a few members of the House of Commons, those that had taken the oath of supremacy, and those that had taken the oath of allegiance, that was to defend the king and his heirs against all conspiracies and attempts whatsoever against his and their persons, their crowns and dignities, not only against the Pope's sentence, as some would pretend, but, as otherwise, against all attempts and conspiracies; not only against his person, crown, and royal dignity, nor Pope's sentence nor, only in order to the profession of religion, but absolutely or otherwise, that is, whatsoever attempts, by any power, authority, or pretence whatsoever. I say, when a few members of the House of Commons, not an eighth part of them, having taken these oaths, shall assume upon themselves an authority; an authority, what to do? Shall assume to themselves an authority to make laws, which was never heard before; authority to make laws: what laws? A law for an High Court of Justice, a law for lives, to sentence men's lives; and whose life? The life of their sovereign: upon such a king who, as to them, had not only redressed long before, at the beginning of the parliament, all grievances that were and were imaginable, taken away the Star Chamber, High Commission Court, and about shipping: such a king, and after such concessions, that he had made in the Isle of Wight, when he had granted so much that was more than the people would have desired. When these few Commons not only without, but excluding, the rest of the Commons; not only without, but excluding the rest but rejecting the Lords too, that then sat: when these few Commons shall take upon them this authority, and, by colour of this, their king, sovereign, liege lord, shall be sentenced, put to death; and that put to death, even as their king, and sentenced as their king; put to death as their king, and this before his own door, even before that place where he used in royal majesty to hear ambassadors, to have his honourable entertainments: that this King shall be thus put to death at noon-day, it is such an aggravation of villainy that, truly, I cannot tell what to say. No story that ever was, I do not think any romance, any fabulous tragedy, can produce the like.

Gentlemen, if any person shall now come and shroud himself under this pretended authority, or such a pretended authority, you must know that this is so far from an excuse that it is the height of aggravation. The Court of Common Pleas is the common shop for justice: in that court an appeal is brought for murder which ought to have been in the [Court of] King's Bench, the Court gives judgment, the party is condemned, and executed: in this case, it is murder in them that executed because they had no lawful authority. I speak this to you to show you that no man can shroud himself by colour of any such false or pretended authority. I have but one thing more to add to you upon this head; and that is (which I should have said at first) if two or more do compass or imagine the king's death, if some of them go on so far as to consultation; if others of them go further, they sentence, and execute, put to death: in this case they are all guilty. The first consultation was treason. I have no more to add, but one particular, a few words.

As you will have bills presented against those for compassing, imagining, adjudging the king: so possibly you may have bills presented against some of those for levying war against the king: levying of war, which is another branch of the statute 25 Edward III. It was but declarative of the common law: it was no new law. By that law it was treason to levy war against the king. But to levy war against the king's authority, you must know, is treason too. If men will take up arms upon any public pretence; if it be to expulse aliens; if but to pull out privy councillors; if it be but against any particular laws, to reform religion, to pull down enclosures: in all these cases, if persons have assembled themselves in a warlike manner to do any of these acts, this is treason, and within that branch of levying war against the king. This was adjudged in the late king's time in Berstead's case, Queen Elizabeth's, Henry VIII's, former times, King James's time: much more; men will go, not only to levy war against the king, but against the laws, all the laws, subvert all the laws, to set up new laws, models of their own. If any of these cases come to be presented to you, you know what the laws are.

To conclude, you are now to enquire of blood, of royal blood, of sacred blood; blood like that of the saints under the altar, crying *Quousque, Domine*? *How long, Lord*, etc. This blood cries for vengeance, and it will not be appeased without a bloody sacrifice.

Remember but this, and I have done: I shall not press you upon your oaths; you are persons of honour; you all know the obligation of an oath. This I will say, that he that conceals or favours the guilt of blood takes it upon himself; wilfully, knowingly, takes it upon himself. And we know, that, when the Jews said, **Let his blood be on us and our seed**, it continued to them and their posterity, to this day. God save the King. Amen, Amen. […]

How long, Lord: A biblical refrain, e.g., Psalm 13:1: "How long, Lord? Will you forget me forever? How long will you hide your face from me?"

Let his blood be on us and our seed: Referencing Matthew 27:25, which was taken as evidence of the Jews' supposed "blood guilt" for the killing of Jesus Christ, an interpretation that long supported anti-Jewish sentiment.

10 October 1660.

Sir John Robinson, Knight, Lieutenant of his Majesty's Tower of London, according to his warrant received, delivered to Mr. Sheriff the prisoners hereafter named; who were (in several coaches) with a strong guard of horse and foot conveyed to Newgate [gaol], and about nine of the clock in the morning, delivered to the keepers of that prison, and thence brought to the Sessions House in the Old Bailey [London's central criminal court], where the Commissioners of **Oyer and Terminer** were in Court assembled, and where their indictment was publicly read by Edward Shelton, Esq., Clerk of the Crown.

Oyer and Terminer: See note on p. 53.

The Court being assembled and silence commanded, the commission of oyer and terminer was again read. After which Sir Hardress Waller, Colonel Thomas Harrison, and Mr. William Heveningham were brought to the bar and commanded to hold up their hands: which Sir Hardress Waller and Mr. Heveningham did; but Harrison, being commanded to hold up his hand, answered, I am here, and said, My Lord, if you please, I will speak a word—

Court: Hold up your hand, and you shall be heard in due time. Mr. Harrison, the course is that you must hold up your hand first.

And then he held up his hand. The indictment was read, purporting; That he, together with others, not having the fear of God before his eyes, and being instigated by the Devil, did maliciously, treasonably, and feloniously, contrary to his due allegiance and bounden duty, sit upon and condemn our late sovereign lord, King Charles the First, of ever blessed memory: and also did upon 30 January 1649 sign and seal a warrant for the execution of his late sacred and serene Majesty of blessed memory. [...]

[Hardress Waller is arraigned, then Thomas Harrison.]

Clerk: Thomas Harrison, how say you? Are you guilty of the treason whereof you stand indicted, and are now arraigned? Or not guilty?

Harrison: My Lords, have I liberty to speak?

Court: No more (at this time) than guilty, or not guilty. Mr. Harrison, you have heard the direction before. We can give you but the same rule. If you plead not guilty, you shall be heard at large: if guilty, you know what remains.

Harrison: Will you give me leave to give you my answer in my own words?

Lord Chief Baron: There is no answer but what the law directs. It is the same with you as with all others, or as I would desire, if I were in your condition. You must plead not guilty: or, if you confess guilty, there must be judgment upon your confession. The same rule for one must be for another.

Harrison: You express your rule very fair, as well to me, as this gentleman (pointing at Sir Hardress Waller) but I have something to say to your Lordships, which concerns your Lordships as well as myself.

Court: You must hold, and plead guilty or not guilty. If you go otherwise (as I told you before) it will be as if you pleaded not at all, and then judgment will pass against you. The law gives the words, frames your answer; it is none else, but the laws: guilty or not guilty.

Harrison: My Lord, I have been kept close prisoner near these three months, that nobody might have access to me. Do you call me to give you a legal answer, not knowing of my trial, till nine o'clock last night, and brought away from the Tower to this place at six o'clock this morning?

Court: You must give your direct answer, guilty or not guilty. You cannot say, it is sudden, or unprovided. You spend time in vain. You trouble the Court. You must plead guilty or not guilty. We must not suffer you to make discourses there. You must plead either guilty or not guilty.

Clerk: Are you guilty? Or not guilty?

Harrison: I am speaking. Shall I not speak two words?

Court: If you will not put yourself upon your trial, you must expect that course that the law directs.

Harrison: May it please your Lordships, I am now—

Clerk: Are you guilty, or not guilty?

Harrison: I desire to be advised by the law. This is a special case.

Court: The law allows nothing now, but to plead guilty or not guilty.

Court: You must plead to your indictment. If it be treason, it cannot be justified; if it be justifiable, it is not treason: Therefore plead guilty or not guilty.

Harrison: Give me advice in this—

Clerk: Thomas Harrison, are you guilty? Or not guilty?

Harrison: I would willingly render an account of all my doings—

Clerk: Are you guilty? Or not guilty?

Court: You have been acquainted with the legal proceedings. You never found in all your experience that any prisoner at the bar for felony or treason was suffered thus to discourse, or to answer otherwise, than guilty or not guilty.

Clerk: Are you guilty, or not guilty?

Mr. Solicitor General: I do beseech your Lordships, he may plead. Peradventure he knows his case so well that he thinks it as cheap to defy the Court as submit to it.

Court: We must enter your **standing mute**: that's judgment.

standing mute: Refusing to enter a plea in court; traditionally sanctioned by "peine forte et dure," being pressed under heavy weights until death or compliance.

Clerk: Are you guilty, or not guilty?

Harrison: Will you refuse to give me any satisfaction—

Court: Are you guilty, or not guilty?

Harrison: Will you give me your advice?

Court: We do give you advice. The advice is: there is no other plea but guilty or not guilty. You shall be heard when you have put yourself upon your trial.

Clerk: Are you guilty, or not guilty?

Harrison: You do deny me counsel, then I do plead not guilty.

Clerk: You plead not guilty. Is this your plea?

Harrison: Yes.

Clerk: How will you be tried?

Harrison: I will be tried according to the laws of the Lord.

Clerk: Whether by God and the Country?

Lord Chief Baron: Now I must tell you: if you do not put yourself upon your Country, you have said nothing.

Clerk: How will you be tried?

Harrison: It is to put myself upon what you please to put me upon.

Court: If you understand (you are not every man, you are versed in proceedings of law) you know, you must put yourself upon the trial of God and your Country. If you do not, it is as good as if you had said nothing.

Harrison: You have been misinformed of me—

Court: You have pleaded not guilty. That which remains is you must be tried by God and the Country: otherwise, we must record your standing mute.

Clerk: How will you be tried?

Harrison: I will be tried according to the ordinary course.

Clerk: Whether by God and the Country? You must speak the words.

Harrison: They are vain words—

Court: We have given you a great deal of liberty and scope, which is not usual. It is the course and proceedings of law: if you will be tried, you must put yourself upon God and the Country.

Clerk: How will you be tried?

Harrison: I do offer myself to be tried in your own way, by God and my Country.

Clerk: God send you a good deliverance. [...]

[Similar arraignments follow for others to be tried, some raising points of law or other objections to the proceedings.]

The Court then adjourned to the same place, till the next morning, seven o'clock.

[...] Proclamation was then made.
If any man can inform my Lords, the king's justices, the king's sergeant, or the king's attorney, before this inquest be taken; let them come forth and they shall

be heard, for now the prisoner stands at the bar upon his deliverance. And all those bound by recognizance to appear, let them come forth and give their evidence, or else to forfeit their recognizance. George Masterson, James Nutley, Robert Coytmore, Holland Simson, and William Jessop, witnesses, were called.

Court: Gentlemen that are not of the jury, pray, clear the passage. The prisoner is here for life and death; let him have liberty to see the jury.

Clerk: Thomas Harrison, hold up thy hand.

Clerk: Look upon the prisoner, you that are sworn. You shall understand that the prisoner at the bar stands indicted by the name of Thomas Harrison, late of Westminster in the county of Middlesex, gentleman; for that he, together with John Lisle, etc. (Here the indictment was read.) Upon which indictment he has been arraigned and thereunto has pleaded not guilty, and for his trial has put himself upon God and the Country: which Country you are. Now your charge is to enquire whether he be guilty of the high treason, in manner and form as he stands indicted, or not guilty. If you find that he is guilty, you shall **enquire what goods and chattels** he had at the time of committing the said treason or at any time since. If you find that he is not guilty, you shall enquire whether he did fly for it: if you find that he fled for it, you shall enquire of his goods and chattels, as if you had found him guilty: if you find, that he is not guilty, nor that he did fly, you shall say so, and no more. And take heed to your evidence.

enquire what goods and chattels: Individuals found guilty of serious crimes (felonies and treasons), or outlawed for evading trial upon such charges, stood to forfeit their property.

Mr. Keeling enforced the charge at large. After whom Sir Heneage Finch, His Majesty's Solicitor General, in these words: May it please Your Lordships, we bring before your Lordships into judgment this day the murderers of a king. A man would think the laws of God and men had so fully secured these sacred persons that the sons of violence should never approach to hurt them. For (My Lord) the very thoughts of such an attempt have ever been presented by all laws, in all ages, and all nations of the world as a most unpardonable treason. My Lord, this is that, that brought the two eunuchs in the Persian Court to their just destruction: *Voluerunt insurgere* [They wished to rise up], **says the text**: and yet that was enough to attaint them. And so (My Lord) it was by the Roman laws too, as Tacitus observes, *Qui deliberant, desciverunt* [Those who consider revolting have already revolted]. To doubt or hesitate in a point of allegiance is direct treason and apostasy. And upon this ground it is, that the statute, upon which your Lordships are now to proceed, has these express words: If a man does compass or imagine the death of the King, etc.

says the text: A story from the biblical book of Esther 2:21–23, in which two royal officials who had conspired to kill their king were executed.

Kings, who are God's vicegerents [deputies] upon Earth, have thus far a kind of resemblance of the Divine Majesty, that their subjects stand accountable to them for the very thoughts of their hearts. Not that any man can know the heart, save God alone, but because when the wicked heart breaks out into any open expressions, by which it may be judged, 'tis the thoughts of the heart which make the treason: the overt act is but the evidence of it.

My Lords, this care and caution is not so to be understood as if it were the single interest of one royal person only. The law doth wisely judge and foresee that upon the life of the king depends the laws and liberties, the estates and properties, the wealth and peace, the religion, and, in sum, the glory of the nation.

My Lords, this judgment of the law has been verified by a sad experience: for when that blessed king (whose blood we are now making inquisition for) was untimely taken away, religion and justice both lay buried in the same grave with him. And there they had slept still, if the miraculous return of our gracious sovereign had not given them a new resurrection.

My Lords, my Lord Coke, in his comment upon this statute, has one conceit, which is somewhat strange; I am sure it is very new: he seems to think that it would have added to the perfection of this law if there had been a time limited for the party to be accused. But certainly the work of this day has quite confuted that imagination. For here is a treason that has so long outfaced the law and the justice of this kingdom that, if there had been any time of limitation in the statute, there would have been no time nor place left for punishment. And, if this treason had but once grown up to an impunity, it might perhaps have drawn the guilt of that innocent blood, and with it the vengeance due to it, upon the whole nation.

The scope of this indictment is for the compassing the death of the king. The rest of the indictment, as the usurping authority over the king's person, the assembling, sitting, judging, and killing of the king, are but so many several overt acts to prove the intention of the heart. We are not bound (under favour) to prove every one of these against every particular person who is indicted: for he that is in at one, is guilty in law of all rest, as much as if he had struck the fatal stroke itself. Nay (under favour) if we can prove any other overt act, besides what is laid in the indictment, as the encouraging of the soldiers to cry out, Justice, Justice; or preaching to them to go in this work as godly and religious; or any other act of all that catalogue of villainies for which the story will be for ever infamous: this may be given in evidence to prove the compassing and imagining the king's death. The conclusion of this indictment alleges the fact done to be to the great displeasure of Almighty God and to the great disgrace of the people of England, a truth so clear and known that it can neither be heightened by any aggravation or lessened by any excuse.

As for the fact itself, with the manner of it, I shall not need to open it at large: for these things were not done in a corner; every true English heart still keeps within itself a bleeding register of this story, only (my Lords) in the way to our evidence, with your Lordships' favour, this, I think, may be fit to be said.

First, for the year 1648[–49], for that was the fatal year of this King, and beyond that year we shall not now enquire, I say whatsoever, in the year 1648[–49 that] could have been done by a parliament to save the life of a king was done in this case. They opened the way to a treaty in spite of the army; and, while these **sons of Zeruiah**, who were too hard for them, were engaged in service in the remoter parts, they hastened the treaty as much as was possible. The debate upon his majesty's concessions were voted a good ground for peace, notwithstanding the Remonstrances of the Army still flew about their ears, and notwithstanding the oppositions of a fearful and unbelieving party of the House of Commons whom the army had frightened into an awful and a slavish dependence upon them. And, when nothing else could be done for him, they were so true to the obligations they lay under, that they resolved to fall with him: and did so. For the army, who saw the treaty proceed so fast, made as great haste to break it. They seize upon the blessed person of our sacred king by force and bring him to London. And here they force the parliament; shut out some members, imprison others: and then called this wretched little company which was left a parliament. By this, and before they had taken upon them the boldness to dissolve the House of Peers, they pass a law and erect, forsooth!, a High Court of Justice, as they call it, a shambles of justice; appoint judges, advocates, officers, and ministers; sit upon the life of the king. Now they speak out and expound their own declarations, and tell us what that was, which before they had demanded in obscure terms, when they called for justice against all delinquents. Now they speak plainly what they mean, and call this blessed king, this glorious saint, the grand delinquent. *Haec acies victum factura nocentem est.* [This battle will make the conquered guilty.]

My Lords, when they had thus proceeded to appoint their judges, officers, and court, then they call this person, their only liege lord and sovereign to the bar, and, by a formal pageantry of justice, proceed to sit upon him, arraign, try, sentence, condemn, and kill (I had almost said crucify) him, whom they could not but know to be their king. And all this against the clearest light, the sharpest checks, and most through convictions of conscience, that ever men resisted. And yet, in this moment of time, such was the majesty and innocence of our gracious sovereign that the people followed him with tears in their eyes and acclamations in their mouths, "God save the King," even then, when the soldiers were ready to fire upon them, who did either look sadly or speak affectionately. And yet it will appear upon our evidence, too, that so few of the very common soldiers could be brought to approve these proceedings, or to cry out justice, that their officers were fain by money, or blows, or both, to bring a great many to it.

My Lords, the actors in this tragedy were many, very many, so many that sure their name is Legion, or rather many **Legions**. And certainly (my Lords) when we shall consider the thing that they have done, we cannot but look upon it as a villainy, which had in it all the ingredients to make it detestable

sons of Zeruiah: Rashly belligerent nephews of the biblical King David, sons of David's sister Zeruiah, who often urged killing as a way to solve a problem, no matter how deceitful or contrary to David's sense of God's will the act might be.

Haec … est: A quote from Lucan's *Pharsalia*, an epic poem written c. 60 CE on the civil war between Julius Caesar and Pompey.

Legions: Refers to the biblical story of a man possessed by many demons who called themselves Legion, "for we are many"; see e.g., Mark 5:9.

that it was possible for the counsel of men, or devils either, to put together. But yet, if anything can be of a deeper dye than the guilt of that sacred blood, wherewith they stand polluted, me thinks their impudence should make them more odious than their treason. It was the destruction of God's anointed, in the name of the Lord. It was the murder of a most blessed and beloved prince, in the name of his people. Him, whom they had taken the transcendent boldness to imprison as the author of the war, they put to death, because he would have been the author of our peace. And that with so much scorn and indignity, that some of them were not ashamed to spit in the face of our lord and sovereign. And when they had thus quenched the light of Israel, darkness and confusion did over-spread the face of the land. Many poor subjects at home, and some Protestants in foreign nations, at the very news of it fell down dead, as if this excellent king had been in a natural as well as a religious sense the breath of our nostrils, the anointed of the Lord, who was **taken in their pits**. The judges, officers, and other immediate actors in this pretended court were in number about fourscore [80]. Of these some four or five and twenty are dead and gone to their own place. The God of recompenses has taken the matter so far into His own hands: and who knows, but that it might be one dreadful part of His vengeance that they died in peace? Some six or seven of them, who are thought to have sinned with less malice, have their lives spared, indeed, but are like to be brought to a severe repentance by future penalties. Some eighteen or nineteen have fled from justice, and wander to and fro about the world with the **mark of Cain** upon them, are perpetual[ly] trembling, lest every eye that sees them and every hand that meets them should fall upon them. Twenty nine persons do now expect your justice. Amongst them the first that is brought is the prisoner at the bar, and he deserves to be the first; for, if any person now left alive ought to be styled the conductor, leader, and captain of all this work, that's the man.

He (my Lord) brought the king up a prisoner from Windsor, but how, and in what manner, with how little duty, nay, with how little civility to a common person, you will hear in time. He sat upon him, sentenced him, he signed the warrant, first to call that court together, then the bloody warrant to cut off his sacred head. Against him, as against all the rest, our evidence will be of two sorts: witnesses, *viva voce*, that shall first prove to your Lordships that every person now in question did sit in that court, when their king stood as a prisoner at the bar. We shall prove that the precept by which this pretended court was summoned was not obeyed and executed, till it had had the hands and seals of most of the pretended judges: among the rest, the hand of the prisoner at the bar will be found there. We shall prove his hand to the bloody warrant, for severing the sacred head of our blessed sovereign from the body, and then some circumstances of his malice, and of his demeanour. And after we have done with our witnesses *viva voce*, if we have occasion to use records of parliament,

taken in their pits: I.e., Taken in their snares or traps, from Lamentations 4:20, a passage describing the destruction of Jerusalem and the suffering of exiled Jews.

mark of Cain: From the Bible's account of God's punishment of Cain for killing his brother, Genesis 4:15, in which God banished Cain but marked him to prevent anyone from killing him.

viva voce: Literally, "with living voice," but here meaning oral testimony.

we shall show them too; for we have the originals or authentic copies. But now we shall proceed to our evidence.

Proclamation was made for silence.

Sir Edward Turner: My Lords, the service of this day does call to my memory the story of good **King Amaziah**. We read in Holy Writ that his father, King Joash, was murdered, and murdered by his own subjects: but we read further, that, when Amaziah had regained the crown [and] was settled in the government, he slew those that slew his father. He did go down into Edom, the Valley of Salt, and there he did slay ten thousand. The work of this day does very much resemble that action. Our good and gracious king, his father of blessed memory and our father, his natural, and our politic[al] father, to whom our natural allegiance was due was murdered, and by his own subjects. But, my lords, this was not a national crime: and our good and gracious sovereign has done us that honour and right to vindicate us in foreign nations. And now [that] he is come home in power and glory, he does continue in the same mind. That's the reason we are not now slain by thousands; but that those miscreants are gathered up here and there that did commit the offence and would have involved the nation in a common infamy.

King Amaziah: A story from the biblical history, 2 Kings 14.

Gentlemen of the jury, your time to enquire of this matter is precious, more precious than my words; else I would repeat to you the history of the tragedy; at least that summary that was entered in the black book, or the journals of that they then called a parliament. It shall suffice to tell you, and that most truly, that it was but a handful of men in respect of the whole nation that did contrive and design this damnable and traitorous plot to subvert the laws and change the government of this well-governed nation. In prosecution of which they did cast abroad and spread forth **Jesuitical** maxims, damnable and diabolical principles, to intoxicate the people. And, when their heads were troubled, they were easily led into arms; where, after some time, they grew drunk with successes. And when they had drunk too much of the loyal blood of the people, then they thirsted for the royal blood also. I do confess, we read in stories that kings have before this time been murdered: some in our nation, as [were] King Richard II and **Edward III**, and in other nations. But the actors of those murders were modest to these. They did it in private; these in the face of the sun and the people. But it was those people, gentlemen, they had corrupted with shares in their robberies and villainies. They pretended it was in a way of justice: but, you must know, no justice can be executed upon the person of the king. Touch not mine anointed, says God himself.

Jesuitical: Jesuits are members of a Roman Catholic society renowned now, as then, for missionary work and education, but particularly feared by early modern English Protestants as insidious agents of the Papacy who lived by morally repugnant maxims, including the belief that the ends justified the means.

Edward III: A mistake for Edward II.

My Lords, I do read in the Roman history, that both amongst them and other nations, there was no law against parricide. It was not thought that any man was so unnatural and devilish to destroy his father. But we do find amongst the Romans such a fact was committed, and then they were at a loss to punish it. The way was this, that they found out: the offender they sewed into a **mail** of leather so close that no water could get in. When they had done, they threw him into the sea, by this denoting [that] the offender was not worthy to tread upon the ground nor to breathe in the air, nor to have the benefit of any of the four elements, nor the use of any of God's creatures: and so he starved.

Gentlemen, parricide and regicide differ not in nature, but in degree. Parricide is the killing of the father of one or a few persons; regicide the killing the father of a country. What punishment then is suitable to this offence? Gentlemen, the prisoner at the bar is accused of this offence and now to be tried by you. But, before we enter upon the evidence, I must, with the leave of the court, inform you that though the indictment contains many circumstances and gradations in the treason, yet the imagining and compassing the death of our late sovereign is the treason to which we shall apply our evidence, this being, both by the common law and by the statute of 25 Edward III the principal treason to be enquired of. And the other circumstances in the indictment are but so many matters to prove the overt act. The consultations; the assuming power to try and to condemn the king; the assault upon him and the fatal blow that was given him, are but so many demonstrations and open acts, proving the first treasonable design of the heart.

It will be enough for you, and so my Lords will tell you, if we prove the treason itself, which is the compassing and imagining the death of the king though we fail in some of the circumstances laid in the indictment. I do not speak this as if we should fail in any: but it is not necessary to prove them all. If we prove any, you are to find the prisoner guilty. I am not willing to hold your lordships too long in the porch, but desire to descend into the body of the business: and so we shall call our witnesses, and doubt not but to prove, that this man at the bar was the first and not the least of these offenders.

Mr. George Masterson was called.

Mr. Harrison: When I was before your lordships yesterday, I offered something very material in reference to the jurisdiction of the court, but you told me according to the rule, I must plead guilty or not guilty, and what I had to offer should be heard in its proper place. I now desire to know, whether it be proper now to deliver myself, before you proceed to the calling of witnesses: for I would go the best way, and would not willingly displease you.

Lord Chief Baron: What was promised you yesterday, God forbid but you should have it. But I think it will be best for you to hear the evidence; and then what you have to say, you shall be fully heard.

Mr. Harrison: I am content.

Whereupon George Masterson, Stephen Kirk, Francis Hearn, William Clark, Robert Coytmore, and James Nutley were called and sworn.

Counsel: Mr. Masterson, whether did the prisoner at the bar sit in that which they called the High Court of Justice to sentence the king, or no? Pray, tell my lords and the jury thereof, and what else you know of the matter.

Mr. Masterson: Upon the oath I have taken (my lords, and gentlemen of the jury) I saw the prisoner, Thomas Harrison, sit in that which they called the High Court of Justice, upon the 27th day of January, in the year 1649, to sentence the king.

Counsel: Was it the day the sentence was passed against the king?

Mr. Masterson: It was the day of the sentence, the 27th of January, 1649.

Counsel: Can you say anything else?

Mr. Masterson: I do (Sir) further remember, that, when the clerk of the court (as he was called) read the sentence against the king and said it was the sentence of the whole court, I saw the prisoner at the bar, together with others, stand up, to my apprehension, as assenting to it.

Counsel: Was there not direction that all should stand up, as assenting?

Mr. Masterson: I do not know that; but, when the sentence was read, several of them did stand up, and he among the rest, as assenting to the sentence, as the spectators understood.

Counsel: Mr. Clark. What do you say to the same question?

Mr. Clark: My lords and gentlemen of the jury, I remember I saw the prisoner at the bar sit several times in the Court of Justice, as they called it, particularly on the 23rd and 27th of January, 1649, as I took notice of it in a book.

Counsel: Was that the day of the sentence?

Mr. Clark: Yes, my lord.

Counsel: What say you to that of the rising of those persons in the court?

Mr. Clark: I remember they all rose; but I did not take particular notice then of the prisoner.

Counsel: Mr. Kirk, you hear the question. Did you see the prisoner at the bar, in Westminster Hall, sitting upon the bench in that, which they called the High Court of Justice, when the king stood prisoner at the bar there?

Mr. Kirk: My Lord, I did see the prisoner at the bar sit several days in that, which they called the High Court of Justice. I was there every day of their sitting.

Counsel: Do you remember he was there on the 27th of January, 1649?

Mr. Kirk: I do, sir.

Counsel: Tell the jury what was the work there.

Mr. Kirk: It was sentence. I did take the names of all those gentlemen that did appear in the court on that day, the 27th of January, 1649, and amongst the rest, I took a note of that gentleman's name, as being present.

Counsel: Whereas these gentlemen (Mr. Masterson and Mr. Clark) have declared that, as assenting to the sentence they all stood up: Did you see them stand? And whether by direction, or no?

Mr. Kirk: As for the direction, I know nothing of it, but the members then present in the court (after sentence was read) as far as my eyes could perceive, stood up unanimously; I suppose, as assenting to the sentence.

Court: Mr. Nutley, did you know the prisoner at the bar? Have you seen him sit in Westminster Hall at any time upon the bench, when the king was brought as a prisoner to the bar?

Mr. Nutley: My lords and gentlemen of the jury, I saw the prisoner at the bar several days sit there, amongst the rest of the judges, as a judge, I suppose. To the best of my remembrance, he sat there four days together.

Court: Was he there upon the day of the sentence?

Mr. Nutley: I did take notes, my lord, that day in the court, and I find he did sit that day.

Court: Do you know anything more of the prisoner at the bar?

Mr. Nutley: Thus much I know concerning the prisoner at the bar, my lord. The first day that they sat in public was (as I remember) the 20th of January, 1649.

Some few days afore that, there was a committee that sat in the Exchequer Chamber, and of that committee the prisoner at the bar was one of the members. I do remember well, it was in the evening, they were lighting candles; they were somewhat private. This gentleman was there, I saw him. For, through the kindness of Mr. Phelps, who was then clerk to that committee, I was admitted, pretending first to speak with the said Mr. Phelps and that I had some business with him, and so (as I said before) I was admitted into the committee chamber. Being there, I did observe some passages fall from the prisoner at the bar; the words were to this purpose. He was making a narrative of some discourses, that passed between his late Majesty and himself, in coming between Windsor and London, or Hurst Castle, I know not well whither. My lord, that passage that I observed to fall from him in that discourse, was this. He said, that the king, as he sat in the coach with him, was importunate to know what they intended to do with him.

Mr. Harrison: In the coach was it?

Mr. Nutley: Yea, sir, it was in the coach. He told the rest of the company (as I said before) that the king asked, What do they intend to do with me? Whether to murder me, or no?

And I said to him, there was no such intention, as to kill him we have no such thoughts. But (said he) the Lord has reserved you for a public example of justice. There is one word more, my lords; and that is this, which I heard from this prisoner at the bar; that the reason and end of their meeting together at that committee was concerning the charge. So much I observed. It was concerning the contracting of the impeachment. I observed that some found fault with the length of that, as it was drawn. They were offering some reasons to contract it, and I heard this prisoner at the bar vent this expression, "Gentlemen, it will be good for us to blacken him, what we can; Pray, let us blacken him," or words to that purpose. I am sure "blacken" was his word.

Mr. Wyndham: Mr. Nutley, you speak of an impeachment. Against whom was that impeachment?

Mr. Nutley: It was against his late majesty, the king.

Counsel: And it was to draw up that impeachment so as to blacken him. Was it so?

Mr. Nutley: Yes, Sir.

Mr. Coytmore sworn.

Mr. Wyndham: Did you see the prisoner at the bar sitting in that, which they called the High Court of Justice, on the day when the king was sentenced, or at any other time? Pray tell my lords and the jury.

Mr. Coytmore: My lords and gentlemen of the jury, I was in that which they called the High Court of Justice three or four times. I saw this gentleman either once, or twice, sitting there.

Counsel: Do you know anything more?

Coytmore: No, really. I came only to hear and see what they were doing, and I did there see him, I think, several days: I am sure, once.

Counsel: Did you see him on the 27th of January, 1649 sitting there, which was the day of the sentence?

Coytmore: I cannot call that to memory.

Counsel: Do you know of any expressions that the king should be an example of judgment?

Coytmore: No, my lords.

Mr. Wyndham: My lord, in the next place, we shall show that instrument that was made under the hand and seal of the prisoner at the bar, as well as others, for execution of the king: that bloody warrant. But first we will ask this witness another question.

Counsel: Did you see the prisoner at the bar sit on the bench, as an ordinary spectator, or as one of the judges?

Coytmore: He was in the court, sitting amongst the rest of the judges, as one of them.

Mr. Solicitor: My lords, we will prove that this prisoner at the bar was one of them that took upon him the conducting of the king, and that the king was in his custody; and to the High Court of Justice also.

The Lord Newburgh sworn.

Counsel: Pray, my lord, give yourself the trouble, to raise your voice, and to tell my lords and the jury what you know of the prisoner at the bar, the part that he acted in bringing up the king.

Lord Newburgh: I was then living at his Majesty's lodge at Bagshot, when the prisoner at the bar brought the king from Hurst Castle to London. He was the person that commanded the whole party. And when the king by the way went to dinner, by his order there were sentries set at every door where he was. When the king had dined, he carried him to Windsor and appointed several of his officers to ride close to the king as he was riding, lest he should make his escape from them.

Counsel: That was an imprisonment itself, and so a treason.

Mr. Wyndham: My Lords, we shall now produce to you two instruments which were made, the one for convening and summoning the assembling of that which they called the High Court of Justice, and show this prisoner's hand and seal to that. And then show you likewise that which was the consummating of all, that bloody warrant for execution of his late majesty of blessed memory, with the hand and seal of the prisoner at the bar unto it, amongst others.

Mr. Solicitor: My lords, it will be fit before this to give you an account of how we came by these instruments.

Mr. Jessop sworn.

Counsel: Show to Mr. Jessop the warrant for summoning that court.

Mr. Solicitor: Mr. Jessop, pray tell my lords and the jury how you came by that instrument you have in your hand.

Mr. Jessop: May it please your lordships, I, having the honour to attend the House of Commons, the House was pleased to make an order that Mr. Scobel should deliver into my hands all such books and records, papers, and other things as did belong to the House of Commons. In pursuance of that order, I did receive, amongst other things, this instrument, as a thing that had been formerly in his hands, as clerk of the House of Commons.

Mr. Solicitor: We desire it may be read, my lords.

Court: Pray first, prove his hand.

Mr. Harrison: I desire to know what is offered to be read.

Court: It is a warrant that you sealed, amongst other pretended judges of your High Court of Justice (as you called it) for trial of the king, for summoning that court.

Counsel: Mr. Kirk, have you seen the hand-writing of the prisoner at any time?

Mr. Kirk: I have very often seen it and am well acquainted with it; and, so far as it's possible a man can testify touching the hand of another person, I do verily believe this to be his hand.

Counsel: How came you to be acquainted with his hand?

Mr. Kirk: As he was a member of the House of Commons, and my employment having relation thereto, I have seen him set his hand several times.

Mr. Farrington sworn.

Counsel: Do you believe that this is the hand-writing of the prisoner at the bar? (The instrument being showed him.)

Mr. Farrington: I did not see him write it, my Lords; but I believe it to be his: for I have often seen his hand-writing. It is his hand, so far as possibly a man can know any person's hand, that did not see him write.

Mr. Harrison: I desire to see the instrument.

Which being showed to him, he said, I believe it is my own hand.

Counsel: That's the warrant for summoning that Court that he owns his hand to.

Court: Show him the other instrument, that being for execution of the sentence.

Mr. Harrison: (It being showed him) I do think this is my hand too.

Counsel: If you think it, the jury will not doubt it. That's the bloody warrant for execution. And we desire they may be both read.

Mr. Harrison: My lords, do these learned gentlemen offer these, as being any records?

Counsel: No, but as your own hand-writing.

Mr. Harrison: If you do not read it as a record, I hope your lordships will not admit of anything of that kind against me.

Counsel: He knows that a letter under his hand and seal may be read in a court. We do not offer it as a record, but prove it by witnesses, that it is your hand-writing.

Court: You have confessed these to be your hands. Whether they are records, or no; whether papers or letters: they may be read against you. You signed the warrant for convening together those which you called the High Court of Justice, and you signed the other warrant for putting the king to death. You do confess these two things. We do not see what further use may be made of them.

Court: You might observe how the indictment was for the imagining, compassing, and contriving the king's death. To prove that, there must be some overt act, and a letter under the party's hand is a sufficient overt act to prove such imagination: to that end these are used.

Mr. Harrison: I do not come to be denying anything that in my own judgment and conscience, I have done or committed, but rather to be bringing it forth to the light.

Court: Sir, you must understand this by the way, this you must take along with you; that these are read, not as anything of authority in themselves, or as used to any other purpose, but as an evidence of the fact against you. Take that along with you. (The two bloody warrants for trial and for execution of His Majesty were here read. […])

Mr. Wyndham: Gentlemen of the jury, we have done our evidence, and you must know, gentlemen, that the principal point of the indictment is for compassing, imagining, and contriving the death of his late majesty of glorious memory. There lies the treason. So says the Statute of 25 Edward III. It has nothing of killing the king there, but of imagining and compassing the death of the king. The going about it, that's the treason, as has been learnedly opened to you. The rest are but overt acts. If there be such an imagination or compassing the death of the king once declared, though no fruit at all follow, it is treason. Here certainly you have a very full evidence given. We show you a consultation; this is one overt act, which would do the work, if there were nothing else. I must tell you (and that with submission to my lords, the justices) if they had advised and gone no further, that had been treason in the letter of the law. They convened and met together, and suppose then, they had absolved and acquitted him; do you think they had absolved themselves from treason? With reverence be it spoken: if they had acquitted him, they had been guilty of treason. Assuming a power to put the king to death is an overt act, declaring such an imagination, you see this prisoner was no ordinary actor in it: his hand is in at all games, taking of him, imprisoning of him, bringing him to London, and setting guards on him. You see also his malice, "Let us blacken him": for they knew his innocence would shine forth, unless it was blackened by their imputations. He sat many times, as you hear, and sentenced him, and assented to that sentence by standing up, and likewise by concluding the catastrophe of that sad beginning of sufferings, his making a warrant for his execution, and accordingly you know what did follow. I think a clearer evidence of a fact can never be given, than is for these things.

(Here the spectators hummed.)

Lord Chief Baron: Gentlemen, this humming is not at all becoming the gravity of this court. Let there be free speaking by the prisoner and counsel. It is more fitting for a stage-play than for a court of justice.

Mr. Harrison: It is now time, my lords, to offer what I have to say? Have these learned gentlemen offered what they will say?

Counsel: We have no more, till he has given us occasion: not for evidence of the fact.

Mr. Harrison: My lords, the matter that has been offered to you, as it was touched, was not a thing done in a corner. I believe the sound of it has been in most nations. I believe the hearts of some have felt the terrors of that presence of God, that was with His servants in those days (however it seems good to Him, to suffer this turn to come on us) and are witnesses, that the things were not done in a corner. I have desired, as in the sight of Him that searches all hearts, whilst this has been done, to wait, and receive from him convictions upon my own conscience, though I have sought it with tears many a time, and prayers, over and over, to that God, to whom you, and all nations, are less than a drop of water of the bucket. And to this moment, I have received rather assurance of it, and that the things that have been done, as astonishing on one hand, I do believe, ere it be long, it will be made known from heaven. There was more from God than men are aware of. I do profess that I would not offer, of myself, the least injury to the poorest man or woman that goes upon the Earth. That I have humbly to offer is this to your lordships: you know what a contest has been in these nations for many years. Divers of those that sit upon the bench, were formerly as active—

Court: Pray Mr. Harrison, do not thus reflect on the Court. This is not to the business.

Mr. Harrison: I followed not my own judgment. I did what I did as out of conscience to the Lord. For when I found those that were as the apple of mine eye to turn aside, I did loath them, and suffered **imprisonment many years**. Rather than to turn, as many did, that did put their hands to this plough, I chose rather to be separated from wife and family, than to have compliance with them, though it was said, Sit at my right hand, and such kind of expressions. Thus I have given a little poor testimony, that I have not been doing things in a corner, or from myself. Maybe, I might be a little mistaken: but I did it all according to the best of my understanding, desiring to make the revealed will of God in his Holy Scriptures as a guide to me. I humbly conceive that what was done, was done in the name of the parliament of England, that what was done, was done by their power and authority, and I do humbly conceive, it is my duty to offer unto you in the beginning, that this court or any court below the High Court of Parliament has no jurisdiction of their actions. Here are many learned in the law and, to shorten the work, I desire I may have the help of counsel learned in the laws that may in this matter give me a little assistance to offer those grounds that the law of the land does offer. I say what was done was done by the authority of the parliament, which was then the supreme authority, and that those that have acted under them are not to be questioned by any power less than them. And, for that I conceive there is much out of the laws to be showed to you, and many precedents also in the case. Much is to be offered to you in that, according to the laws of the nations, that was a due parliament. Those commissions were issued forth, and what was done, was done by their power. And whereas it has been said, we did assume and usurp an authority; I say, this was done rather in the fear of the Lord.

Court: Away with him. Know where you are, Sir. You are in the assembly of Christians. Will you make God the author of your treasons and murders? Take heed where you are: Christians must not hear this. We will allow you to say for your own defence what you can. And we have, with a great deal of patience, suffered you to sally out: wherein you have not gone about so much for extenuation of your crimes, as to justify them, to fall upon others, and to blaspheme God and commit a new treason. For your having of counsel: this is the reason for allowing of counsel, when a man would plead anything, because he would plead it in formality, counsel is allowed. But you must first say in what the matter shall be, and then you shall have the court's answer.

imprisonment many years: When Oliver Cromwell took on the near-kingly powers of Lord Protector, Harrison fell out with him and was imprisoned a few times over the coming years for his opposition to Cromwell's regime.

Lord Finch: Though my lords here have been pleased to give you a great latitude, this must not be suffered, that you should run into these damnable excursions, to make God the author of this damnable treason committed.

Mr. Harrison: I have two things to offer to you, to say for my defence in matter of law. One is that this that has been done, was done by a parliament of England, by the Commons of England assembled in parliament. That being so, whatever was done by their commands or their authority is not questionable by your lordships, as being (as I humbly conceive) a power inferior to that of a High Court of Parliament. That's one. A second is this: That what therefore any did in obedience to that power and authority, they are not to be questioned for it, otherwise we are in a most miserable condition, bound to obey them that are in authority and yet to be punished if obeyed. We are not to judge what is lawful or what is unlawful. My lords, upon these two points I do desire, that those that are learned in the laws may speak, too, on my behalf. It concerns all my countrymen. There are cases alike to this, you know, in King Richard ii's time, wherein some question had been of what had been done by a parliament; and what followed upon it, I need not urge in it. I hope it will seem good to you, that counsel may be assigned, for it concerns all my countrymen.

Counsel: You are mistaken, if you appeal to your countrymen. They will cry you out and shame you.

Mr. Harrison: Maybe so, my Lords, some will; but I am sure others will not.

Mr. Solicitor General: These two points, my lords, are but one, and they are a new treason at the bar, for which he deserves to die, if there were no other indictment. It is the malice of his heart to the dignity and Crown of England. I say this is not matter for which counsel can be assigned. Counsel cannot put into form that which is not matter pleadable itself. It is so far from being true that this was the Act of the supreme parliament of the people of England, that there was nothing received with more heart-bleeding, than this bloody business. But that the world may not be abused by the insinuations of a man who acts as if he had a spirit, and in truth is possessed, I will say: That the Lords and Commons are not a parliament: that the king and Lords cannot do anything without the Commons; nor the king and Commons without the Lords; nor the Lords and Commons without the king, especially against the king. If they do, they must answer it with their head: for the king is not accountable to any coercive power. And for the prisoner to justify his act as if it were the Act of the Commons of England, he is very much to be reproved. Shall he pretend that one House, nay the eighth part of a House (for so it was) can condemn a king, when both Houses cannot condemn one man in spite of the king? I desire, my lords, it may pass with a due reproach and a sentence upon it.

Lord Chief Baron: It is true, your questions are but one point. You pretend the parliament's authority; and, when you come to speak of it, you say the Commons of England. They were but one house of parliament. The parliament? What is that? It is the king, the Lords, and the Commons. I would fain know of you wherever you read, by the light you say you have in your conscience, that the Commons of England were a parliament of England, that the Commons in parliament used a legislative power alone. Do you call that a parliament that sat when the House was purged, as they call it, and was so much under the awe of the army who were then, but forty or forty five at most? Then you say, It was done by authority of them. You must know, where there is such an authority (which indeed is no authority) he that confirms such an authority, he commits a double offence. Therefore consider what your plea is. If your plea were doubtful, we should and ought and would ourselves be of counsel for you. That which you speak concerning conviction of your own conscience, remember, that it is said in Scripture, that they shall think they did God good service when they slay you, as it is in **St. John**. He has a great deal of charity that thinks that what you did was out of a conscientious principle. It was against the light of noon day and common practice. You make yourself a solicitor in the business. Let us blacken him, as much as we can. I have not touched at all upon the evidence. I will not urge it now. I say you justify it upon convictions of conscience, and pretend it upon authority. A thing never known or seen under the sun, that the Commons, nay a few commons alone, should take upon them and call themselves the parliament of England. We have been cheated enough by names and words: there is no colour for what you say. I do think and hope my brethren will speak to this case, that none of us do own that convention, whatsoever it be, to be the parliament of England. There was another aggravation: at this time, that this pretended authority usurped that power, the lords were then sitting. You had not taken this usurped power to dissolve these lords. No; you did this act in despite of the lords, you had sent up an ordinance to the lords, and they rejected it, and thereupon these members took it upon themselves. Amongst those there were some negatives, and those members were under the awe and power of your forces at that time. What you plead, the court are of opinion, tends to the subversion of the laws; for you to usurp power over the people without their consents, to call this the people. We never knew the like before. But the parliament of England was the king, Lords, and Commons. For you to speak of this power and justify this power is an aggravation adding one sin and treason to another. We shall tell you that neither both Houses of Parliament, if they had been there, not any single person, community, not the people, either collectively or representatively, had any colour to have any coercive power over

St. John: From John 16:2: "They shall put you out of the synagogues; yea, the time comes, that whosoever kills you will think that he does God service."

their king. And this plea, which you have spoken of, it ought to be over-ruled, and not to stand good.

Mr. Annesley: I do the more willingly speak to this business because I was one of those that should have made up that parliament that this prisoner pretends to. I was one of that corrupt majority (as they called it) that were put out of the house. He cannot forget that at that time there were guards upon both houses of parliament to attend them, that were of their own appointment: and that those guards were forcibly removed by the prisoner at the bar and his fellows: and other guards put there, who instead of being a defence unto them, when those commons stood at the door, were by them threatened. Yet the Lords and Commons of England in parliament assembled, a full House of Commons, did resolve, notwithstanding what was aforesaid, that the treaty in the Isle of Wight was a ground for peace. Afterwards the major part of the House of Commons, having resolved on this, sent it up to the Lords: that very day when they were adjourned, there were forces drawn down to the House of Commons' door, and none suffered to come into the house, but those that they pleased. All those that had a mind for peace, that minded their duty and trust and allegiance to their king, were seized on by this gentleman and his fellows. When this was done, what did he and those fellows do? They sat and put a check upon all that should come in. None must come in, but those that would renounce their allegiance and duty to their king and the people, for whom they served, and then declared against that vote, which had been passed upon debate of twelve or fourteen hours, and then to call this an House of Commons, nay the supreme authority of the nation, he knows is against the laws of the land. For the House of Commons alone cannot so much as give an oath. It has not power of judicature of life and death: this he knows well to be according to the laws of England. He knows that no authority less than an Act of parliament can make a law, and he knows an Act of parliament must be passed by the king, Lords, and Commons. I wonder much to hear a justification in this kind by one that knows the laws of England so well. There will none of the court allow that that was a parliament. The majority of that house did all disavow it. These things have been already discoursed of: I shall only say, that he, knowing the laws so well, I hope, he shall suffer for transgression thereof.

Mr. Hollis: You do very well know, that this, that you did, this horrid, detestable act which you committed, could never be perfected by you, until you had broken the parliament. That House of Commons, which you say gave you authority, you know, what yourself made of it, when you pulled out the Speaker. Therefore do not make the parliament to be the author of your black crimes. It was innocent of it. You know yourself, what esteem you had of it, when you broke and tore it in sunder, when you scattered and made them hide themselves, to preserve them from your fury and violence. Do not make the parliament to be the author of your crimes. The parliament are the three estates. It must not be admitted, that one house, part of the parliament, should be called the supreme authority. You know what that Rump, that you left did, what laws they made. Did you go home to advise with your country, that chose you for that place? You know that no Act of parliament is binding but what is acted by king, Lords, and Commons. And now, as you would make God the author of your offence, so likewise you would make the people guilty of your opinion. But your plea is overruled.

To which the Court assented.

Mr. Harrison: I was mistaken a little. Whereas it was said, the points were one: I do humbly conceive, they were not so. I say what was done, was done in obedience to the authority. If it were but an order of the House of Commons, thus under a force, yet this court is not judge of that force. I say, if it was done by one estate of parliament, it is not to be questioned.

Court: It was not done by one estate. They were but a part; nay, but an eighth part.

Denzel Holles: It was not a House of Commons. They kept up a company by the power of the sword. Do not abuse the people in saying it was done by the supreme power.

Counsel: My lord, if it were House of Commons, neither House of Commons, nor House of Lords, nor House of Lords and Commons together: no authority upon earth can give authority for murdering the king. This, that he alleges, is treason. My lord, this, that is said, is a clear evidence of that which is charged: there is only this more in it, he has done it, and, if he were to do it again, he would do it.

Lord Chief Baron: It is clear as the noon day that this was not the House of Commons. Suppose it had been a House of Commons, and full, and suppose, (which far be it from me to suppose) they should have agreed upon such a murderous act: for the House of Commons to do such an act, it was void in itself; nay, any authority, without the House of Lords and king, is void. You plead to the jurisdiction of the court, whether we should judge it or not. Yes, I tell you, and proper too. We shall not speak what power we have. The judges have power, after laws are made, to go upon the interpretation of them. We are not to judge of those things that the parliament do. But when the parliament is purged (as you call it) for the Commons alone to act, for you to say, that this is the authority of parliament, it is that, which every man will say, entrenches highly upon his liberty and privilege. And what you have said to your justification, what does it tend to, but as much as this, I did it, justify it, and would do it again: which is a new treason. The greatest right that ever the House of Commons did claim is but over the Commons. Do they claim a particular right over the Lords? Nay, over the king? Make it out, if you can: but it cannot possibly be made out. What you have said aggravates your crimes. It is such an approvement of your treason, that all evidences come short of it. King, Lords, and Commons is the ground of the English law. Without that, no Act of parliament binds.

Justice Mallet: I have been a parliament-man as long as any man here present, and I did never know or hear that the House of Commons had jurisdiction over any, saving their own members: which is as much as I will say concerning the parliament. I have heard a story of a mute, that was born mute, whose father was slain by a stranger, a man unknown. After twenty years or thereabouts, this mute-man fortuned to see the murderer of his father: and these were his words, "Oh! here is he, that slew my father." Sir, the king is the father of the country, *Pater Patria*: so says Sir Edward Coke. He is *Caput Reipublicae,* the head of the commonwealth. Sir, what have you done? Here you have cut off the head of the whole commonwealth, and taken away him that was our father, the governor of the whole country. This you shall find printed and published in a book of the greatest lawyer, Sir Edward Coke. I shall not need, my lord, to say more of this business. I do hold the prisoner's plea vain and unreasonable, and to be rejected.

Justice Hyde: I shall not trouble you with many words. I am sorry that any man should have the face and boldness to deliver such words as you have. You, and all, must know that the king is above the two houses. They must propose their laws to him. The laws are made by him and not by them: by their consenting; but they are his laws. That which you speak as to the jurisdiction: you are here indicted for high treason, for you to come to talk of justification of this by pretence of authority, your plea is naught, illegal, and wicked, and ought not to be allowed. As to having of counsel: the Court understands what you are upon: Counsel is not to be allowed in that case, and therefore your plea must be overruled.

Mr. Justice Twisden: I shall agree with that, which many have already said; only this, you have eased the jury; you have confessed the fact. I am of the same opinion, that you can have no counsel. Therefore I overrule your plea, if it had been put in never so good form and manner.

Earl of Manchester: I beseech you, my lords, let us go some other way to work——

Sir William Wild: That which is before us is whether it be a matter of law or fact? For the matter of law, your lordships have declared what it is, his justification is as high a treason as the former. For matter of fact, he has confessed it. I beseech you, my lord, direct the jury for their verdict. This gentleman has forgotten their barbarousness: they would not hear their king.

Court: No counsel can be allowed to justify a treason: that this is a treason, you are indicted by an Act of 25 Edward III. That which you speak of the House of Commons is but part of the House of Commons. They never did, nor had any power, to make a law but by king, Lords, and Commons: and therefore your plea is naught, and all the Court here is of the same opinion. If they were not, they would say so: therefore what you have said is overruled by the Court. Have you anything else to offer?

Mr. Harrison: Notwithstanding the judgment of so many learned ones, that the kings of England are no ways accountable to the parliament. The Lords and Commons in the beginning of this war having declared the king's beginning war upon them; the God of Gods—

Court: Do you render yourself so desperate that you care not what language you let fall? It must not be suffered.

Mr. Harrison: I would not willingly speak to offend any man: but I know God is no respecter of persons. His setting up his standard against the people——

Court: Truly, Mr. Harrison, this must not be suffered: this does not at all belong to you.

Mr. Harrison: Under favour, this does belong to me. I would have abhorred to have brought him to account, had not the blood of Englishmen, that had been shed—

Counsel: Me thinks he should be sent to **Bedlam**, till he comes to the gallows to render an account of this. This must not be suffered. It is in a manner a new impeachment of this king, to justify their treasons against his late Majesty.

Bedlam: An institution to house people deemed insane (a corruption of Bethlem Royal Hospital).

Mr. Solicitor General: My Lords, I pray that the jury may go together upon the evidence.

Sir Edward Turner: My Lords, this man has the plague all over him: it is a pity any should stand near him, for he will infect them. Let us say to him, as they use to write over a house infected, "The Lord have mercy upon him," and so let the officer take him away.

Lord Chief Baron: Mr. Harrison, we are ready to hear you again: but to hear such stuff, it cannot be suffered. You have spoken that which is as high a degree of blasphemy, next to that against God, as I have heard. You have made very ill use of these favours that have been allowed you to speak: your own conscience cannot but tell you the contradiction of your actions against this that you have heard as the opinion of the Court. To extenuate your crimes you may go on; but you must not go as before.

Mr. Harrison: I must not speak so, as to be pleasing to men: but, if I must not have liberty, as an English man——

Court: Pray, do not reflect thus. You have had liberty, and more than any prisoner in your condition can expect: and I wish you had made a good use of it. Keep to the business; say what you will.

Mr. Harrison: My Lords; thus. There was a discourse by one of the witnesses that I was at the committee preparing the charge, and that I should say, "Let us blacken him." The thing is utterly untrue. I abhorred the doing of anything touching the blackening of the king. There was a little discourse between the king and myself. The king had told me that he had heard that I should come privately to the Isle of Wight to offer some injury to him. But I told him I abhorred the thoughts of it. And whereas it is said that my carriage [behaviour] was hard to him, when I brought him to London: it was not I that brought him to London. I was commanded by the General to fetch him from Hurst Castle. I do not remember any hard carriage towards him.

Court: Mr. Harrison, you have said that you deny that of blackening which the witness has sworn, and somewhat else touching the king in his way to London: that the witness has sworn to also. The jury must consider of it, both of their oaths and your contradictions. If you have nothing more to say which tends to your justification, we must direct the jury. The end of your speech is nothing, but to infect the people.

Mr. Harrison: You are uncharitable in that.

Justice Foster: My Lords, this ought not to come from the bar to the bench; if you sally out thus about your conscience. If your conscience should be a darkened conscience, that must not be the rule of other men's actions. What you speak of that nature is nothing to the business. If you have anything to say by way of excuse for yourself for matter of fact, you may speak: but, if you will go on as before, it must not be suffered.

Mr. Harrison: The things that have been done, have been done upon the stage, in the sight of the sun—

Court: All this is a continuance of the justification, and confession of the fact. We need no other evidence.

Counsel: He has confessed his fact, my lords. The matter itself is treason upon treason. Therefore we pray, [give] direction to the jury.

Lord Chief Baron: Mr. Harrison, I must give direction to the jury if you will not go further touching the fact.

Mr. Harrison: My lords, I say, what I did was by the supreme authority. I have said it before, and appeal to your own consciences, that this court cannot call me to question.

Lord Chief Baron: Mr. Harrison, you have appealed to our consciences. We shall do that which by the blessing of God shall be just, for which we shall answer before the tribunal of God. Pray, take heed of an obdurate, hard heart and a seared conscience.

Mr. Harrison: My lords, I have been kept six months a close prisoner and could not prepare myself for this trial by counsel. I have got here some Acts of parliament of that House of Commons, which your lordships will not own; and the proceedings of that house, whose authority I did own.

Lord Chief Baron: This you have said already. If you show never so many of that nature, they will not help you. You have heard the opinion of the court touching that authority. They all unanimously concur in it.

Gentlemen of the jury, you see that this prisoner at the bar is indicted for compassing, imagining, and contriving the death of our late sovereign lord, King Charles I, of blessed memory. In this indictment there are several things given, but as evidences of it: they are but the overt acts of it. The one is, first, that they did meet and consult together about putting the king to death. That alone, if nothing else had been proved in the case, was enough for you to find the indictment. For the imagination alone is treason by the law. But because the compassing and imagining the death of the king is secret in the heart, and no man knows it but God Almighty: I say, that the imagination is treason: yet it is not such as the law can lay hold of, unless it appear by some overt act. Then the first overt act is their meeting, consulting, and proposing to put the king to death. The second is more open; namely, their sitting together, and assuming an authority to put the king to death. The third is sentencing the king. And I must tell you, that any one of these acts prove the indictment. If you find him guilty but of any one of them, either consulting, proposing, sitting, or sentencing (though there is full proof for all) yet notwithstanding you ought to find the indictment. You have heard what the witnesses have said, and the prisoner's own confession. Witnesses have sworn their sitting together and that he was one. One swears he sat four times; another twice; some several times. There are several witnesses for this: as Mr. Masterson, Mr. Clark, Mr. Kirk, and Mr. Nutley. And then you have another thing, too, which truly the prisoner did not speak of. Witness was given against him that he was the person that conducted the king. This was before that, which he would have to be done by a legislative power: and that is another overt act.

If a man will go about to imprison the king, the law knows what is the sad effect of such imprisonment. That has often been adjudged to be an evidence of imagining and compassing the death of the king. That man, the prisoner at the bar, it has been proved to you did imprison the king: and it appears by his own hand to the warrant for summoning of that traitorous assembly, the High Court of Justice, as they called it. And also it appears by his hand to the warrant for execution, that bloody warrant. He has been so far from denying, that he has justified these actions. The evidence is so clear and pregnant as nothing more. I think you need not go out.

The jury went together at the bar, and presently unanimously agreed on their verdict, whereupon they were demanded by the clerk:

Clerk: Are you agreed upon your verdict?

Jury: Yes.

Clerk: Who shall say for you?

Jury: Our foreman. (Which was Sir Thomas Allen.)

Clerk: Thomas Harrison. Hold up thy hand. Gentlemen of the jury, look upon the prisoner. How say you? Is he guilty of the treason whereof he stands indicted and has been arraigned? Or not guilty?

Foreman: Guilty.

Then the keeper was charged to look to the prisoner.

Clerk: What goods and chattels had he at the time of committing this treason, or at any time since?

Foreman: None to our knowledge.

Which verdict being repeated to the jury by Mr. Clerk of the Crown, the jury owned it unanimously.

Mr. Solicitor General: My Lords, upon this verdict, that has been given against the prisoner at the bar, I humbly move that we may have judgment given. Your sessions will be long and your work will be great; his demeanour has been such that he does not deserve a reprieve for so many days as you are like to spend in this session.

Court: Mr. Harrison, they desire judgment upon the verdict. What do you say for yourself, why judgment should not pass against you?

Clerk: Thomas Harrison, hold up thy hand. What have you to say for yourself, why judgment should not pass against you, to die according to law?

Mr. Harrison: I have nothing further to say. Because the Court have not seen meet to hear what was in my heart to speak, I submit to it.

The crier made proclamation for silence whilst judgment was in giving.

Lord Chief Baron: You, that are the prisoner at the bar, you are to pass the sentence of death; which sentence is this. The judgment of this Court is, and the Court does award, that you be led back to the place from whence you came, and from thence to be drawn upon a hurdle to the place of execution, and there you shall be hanged by the neck, and being alive shall be cut down, and your privy-members to be cut off, your entrails to be taken out of your body, and (you living) the same to be burnt before your eyes, and your head to be cut off, your body to be divided into four quarters, and your head and quarters to be disposed of at the pleasure of the king's majesty: and the Lord have mercy upon your soul.

Accounts of the trials of the other regicides follow in the original. Harrison was executed two days later, on 13 October, in just the manner the Lord Chief Baron prescribed. His executioners tossed his severed head into the hurdle that dragged to his own execution John Cooke, the solicitor general who had prosecuted Charles at trial. Both their heads were then set up on poles at Westminster Hall and the quarters of their bodies affixed to the City of London's gates. Ten men in total were executed as regicides in mid-October. Even hostile observers noted that Harrison died unrepentant; his biographer, David Farr, argues that Harrison's resolve helped hasten the end of the executions. He cites one observer's report that while vast crowds attended the executions, "and all people seemed pleased with the sight, yet the odiousness of the crime grew at last to be so much flattened by the frequent executions, and by most of those who suffered dying with much firmness and show of piety, justifying all they had done, not without a seeming joy for their suffering on that account, that the king was advised not to proceed farther."[2]

A work published anonymously by a sympathetic contemporary gives accounts of the executions of Harrison and his fellows: *The Speeches and Prayers of Some of the Late King's Judges ... together with Several Occasional Speeches and Passages on their Imprisonment* (London, 1660). While we cannot be wholly confident of their accuracy, no one challenged them as lies when the suspected publishers were brought to court on charges of sedition. The work has Harrison's purported words from the scaffold, thanking God for accounting him "worthy to be instrumental in so glorious a work" and insisting that "If I had ten thousand lives, I would freely and cheerfully lay them down all to witness to this matter."

---

2 David Farr, *Major-General Thomas Harrison: Millenarianism, Fifth Monarchism and the English Revolution, 1616–1660* (Farnham: Ashgate, 2014), 55.

GLOSSARY OF KEY FIGURES AND TERMS

Agreement of the People: a manifesto prepared by Agitators (i.e., representatives of rank-and-file soldiers in the New Model Army) and civilian Levellers, setting out the fundamentals of a proposed constitution for the postwar government; first issued in October 1647 and then in amended versions thereafter.

Cavaliers: sometimes used broadly to refer to the Royalist party in the civil wars, but also more narrowly to refer to the more nobly born members of the Royalist camp with a lifestyle and mores denounced by their opponents as extravagant and frivolous.

Coke, Sir Edward: a barrister, judge, and respected legal writer who first came to prominence in the reign of Queen Elizabeth. An able defender of royal prerogative in some respects, he was nonetheless dismissed as Chief Justice by King James. Thereafter he turned to work in parliament, helping to prepare the Petition of Right presented to King Charles. His *Institutes of the Laws of England* and published series of law reports ensured him a lasting legacy, despite King Charles's attempts to hinder the publication of some.

Contumacy: a punishable contempt for or obstinate refusal to obey a court's order.

Cromwell, Oliver: an MP who rose to prominence as cavalry commander in the civil wars, and was second-in-command of the parliamentary forces at the time of the king's trial. Soon after the trial, Cromwell replaced Lord Fairfax as the army general and helped force the integration of Ireland and Scotland into the new Commonwealth. In 1653, he closed the Rump Parliament and became Lord Protector. At his death in 1658, he was very briefly succeeded by his eldest son. Assessments of Cromwell and his historical significance diverge widely, with some seeing him as a military dictator but others seeing him as a champion of parliamentary governance. Exhumed and posthumously executed at the restoration of monarchy in 1660, he is now commemorated with a statute outside the Houses of Parliament.

Demurrer: to demur means to object; a demurrer is a legal pleading that even if the alleged facts are true, no legal basis for a court case exists.

Independents: a loose grouping rather than a political party, the Independents were one of two broad factions that emerged within the parliamentary side in the years of fighting, set against the Presbyterians in advocating more complete religious toleration and the separation of Church and State, whereas the Presbyterians wanted to replace one national church with another.

Levellers: a political movement that emerged in the civil war years, with proponents accused (somewhat inaccurately) of trying to level social hierarchies but who did advocate extended voting rights, a free press, equality before the law, and other ostensibly "liberal" rights. Leveller agitation became especially powerful through the New Model Army, until Cromwell had Leveller-inspired mutinies crushed throughout April and May 1649.

Magna Carta: a charter of liberties forced from King John in 1215 by his rebellious barons, and from 1225 endorsed (in modified form) by subsequent kings. Sir Edward Coke did much to retrieve and reinterpret Magna Carta as symbol against tyranny and a manifesto of rights that placed law above even kings while guaranteeing "due process" for all.

Norman Conquest: the invasion and conquest of Anglo-Saxon England led by Duke William of Normandy (in what is now northern France) in 1066. Early modern writers argued about the legal significance of this Conquest, with some writing of a "Norman Yoke" and the need to return to pre-Conquest laws and customs.

Remonstrance: the New Model Army's manifesto of November 1648, setting out its case for parliament to abandon negotiations with King Charles and to move to a trial.

Rump: the derogatory name given to what remained of the House of Commons after Colonel Pride and his men purged it of its more moderate and Presbyterian members on 6 December 1648.

SELECT BIBLIOGRAPHY

Barber, Sarah. *Regicide and Republicanism: Politics and Ethics in the English Revolution, 1646–1659*. Edinburgh: Edinburgh UP, 1998.

Burgess, Glenn, and Matthew Festenstein, ed. *English Radicalism, 1550–1850*. Cambridge: Cambridge UP, 2007.

Carlton, Charles. *Going to the Wars: The Experience of the British Civil Wars, 1638–1651*. London: Routledge, 1992.

Cressy, David. *England on Edge: Crisis and Revolution, 1640–1642*. Oxford: Oxford UP, 2006.

Donagan, Barbara. "Atrocity, War Crime, and Treason in the English Civil War." *American Historical Review* 99 (1994): 1137–66.

Donagan, Barbara. *War in England, 1642–1649*. Oxford: Oxford UP, 2008.

Gentles, Ian. *The English Revolution and the Wars of the Three Kingdoms*. Harlow: Pearson Longman, 2007.

Holmes, Clive. "The Trial and Execution of Charles I." *Historical Journal* 53 (2010): 289–310.

Hughes, Ann. *Gender and the English Revolution*. London: Routledge, 2012.

Kelsey, Sean. "The Death of Charles I." *Historical Journal* 45 (2002): 727–54.

Kelsey, Sean. "The Trial of Charles I." *English Historical Review* 118 (2003): 585–616.

Knoppers, Laura Lunger. *Historicizing Milton: Spectacle, Power and Poetry in Restoration England*. Athens: U of Georgia P, 1994.

Knoppers, Laura Lunger, ed. *The Oxford Handbook of Literature and the English Revolution*. Oxford: Oxford UP, 2012.

Morrill, John, ed. *The Oxford Illustrated History of Tudor and Stuart Britain*. Oxford: Oxford UP, 1996.

Morrill, John. *Stuart Britain: A Very Short Introduction*. Oxford: Oxford UP, 2000.

Nenner, Howard. "The Trial of the Regicides: Retribution and Treason in 1660." In *Politics and the Political Imagination in Later Stuart Britain*, edited by Howard Nenner, 21–42. Woodbridge: Boydell & Brewer, 1998.

Orr, D. Alan. *Treason and the State*. Cambridge: Cambridge UP, 2002.

Peacey, Jason, ed. *The Regicides and the Execution of Charles I*. Basingstoke: Palgrave Macmillan, 2001.

Peacey, Jason. *Print and Public Politics in the English Revolution*. Cambridge: Cambridge UP, 2013.

Robertson, Geoffrey. *The Tyrannicide Brief: The Story of the Man who Sent Charles I to the Scaffold*. London: Chatto & Windus, 2005.

Russell, Conrad. *The Causes of the English Civil War*. Oxford: Oxford UP, 1990.

Russell, Conrad. *The Fall of the British Monarchies, 1637–1642*. Oxford: Oxford UP, 1991.

Scott, Jonathan. *Commonwealth Principles: Republican Writing of the English Revolution*. Cambridge: Cambridge UP, 2004.

Underdown, David. *Pride's Purge*. Oxford: Oxford UP, 1971.

Wedgwood, C.V. *A King Condemned: The Trial and Execution of Charles I*. London: I.B. Tauris, 2011; first ed. 1964.

Worden, Blair. *God's Instruments: Political Conduct in the England of Oliver Cromwell*. Oxford: Oxford UP, 2012.

From the Publisher

A name never says it all, but the word "Broadview" expresses a good deal of the philosophy behind our company. We are open to a broad range of academic approaches and political viewpoints. We pay attention to the broad impact book publishing and book printing has in the wider world; we began using recycled stock more than a decade ago, and for some years now we have used 100% recycled paper for most titles. Our publishing program is internationally oriented and broad-ranging. Our individual titles often appeal to a broad readership too; many are of interest as much to general readers as to academics and students.

Founded in 1985, Broadview remains a fully independent company owned by its shareholders—not an imprint or subsidiary of a larger multinational.

For the most accurate information on our books (including information on pricing, editions, and formats) please visit our website at www.broadviewpress.com. Our print books and ebooks are also available for sale on our site.

On the Broadview website we also offer several goods that are not books—among them the Broadview coffee mug, the Broadview beer stein (inscribed with a line from Geoffrey Chaucer's *Canterbury Tales*), the Broadview fridge magnets (your choice of philosophical or literary), and a range of T-shirts (made from combinations of hemp, bamboo, and/or high-quality pima cotton, with no child labor, sweatshop labor, or environmental degradation involved in their manufacture).

All these goods are available through the "merchandise" section of the Broadview website. When you buy Broadview goods you can support other goods too.

broadview press

www.broadviewpress.com